A BEGINNER'S GUIDE TO *Perfection*

The Definitive Guide for Taking Charge of Your Experience of Life

DAVID J. SAFFOLD

WestBow Press
A DIVISION OF THOMAS NELSON & ZONDERVAN

Copyright © 2017 David J. Saffold.

All rights reserved. No part of this book may be used or reproduced by any means, graphic, electronic, or mechanical, including photocopying, recording, taping or by any information storage retrieval system without the written permission of the author except in the case of brief quotations embodied in critical articles and reviews.

Scripture taken from the New King James Version®. Copyright © 1982 by Thomas Nelson. Used by permission. All rights reserved.

This book is a work of non-fiction. Unless otherwise noted, the author and the publisher make no explicit guarantees as to the accuracy of the information contained in this book and in some cases, names of people and places have been altered to protect their privacy.

WestBow Press books may be ordered through booksellers or by contacting:

WestBow Press
A Division of Thomas Nelson & Zondervan
1663 Liberty Drive
Bloomington, IN 47403
www.westbowpress.com
1 (866) 928-1240

Because of the dynamic nature of the Internet, any web addresses or links contained in this book may have changed since publication and may no longer be valid. The views expressed in this work are solely those of the author and do not necessarily reflect the views of the publisher, and the publisher hereby disclaims any responsibility for them.

Any people depicted in stock imagery provided by Thinkstock are models, and such images are being used for illustrative purposes only. Certain stock imagery © Thinkstock.

ISBN: 978-1-9736-1109-7 (sc)
ISBN: 978-1-9736-1108-0 (hc)
ISBN: 978-1-9736-1110-3 (e)

Library of Congress Control Number: 2017919258

Print information available on the last page.

WestBow Press rev. date: 12/20/2017

CONTENTS

Acknowledgments vii
Introduction ix
Chapter 1 The Great Law of the Universe—As You
           Believe, It Is Done unto You 1
Chapter 2 Destructive Beliefs 29
Chapter 3 Your Personal World 75
Chapter 4 Accessing Your Personal Power 97
Chapter 5 Expanding Your Personal Power 123
Chapter 6 Challenging Your Destructive Beliefs 141
Chapter 7 Rebirth 157
Chapter 8 Perfection 179

ACKNOWLEDGMENTS

I want to acknowledge and give my warm thanks to the family, friends, and teachers that helped me make this book a reality:

My beautiful wife, Kim Saffold, whose love, trust, and support made this entire project possible.

My son, Isaac Saffold, the grammar expert of the family.

My great friend Tom Bridwell for his professional literary editing and insights.

My wonderful friend Helen Eaves for saving me from a personal pronoun nightmare.

My angelic friend and former classmate at The Estuary, Wanda Johnson, whose experience, help, and encouragement helped get me started.

My Mrs. Sunshine, Susan Austin Crumpton, director of The Estuary and my master teacher through six years of intensive study in the healing arts. Thank you for showing me the path to perfection!

And to all those who let me be a part of their journey to new and better experiences of life.

INTRODUCTION

Over the past twenty-five years, I have dramatically changed every aspect of my experience of life, relationships, career, and financial, emotional, and physical health. I have also helped many do the same in their lives using the same process I had used. This book is the culmination of meticulous research and analysis of the psychology and methodology used to successfully implement these desired life changes. The detailed methodology outlined in this book will work equally well for the person who finds himself or herself lying at death's doorstep in the grips of severe alcohol and drug addiction or the person who simply desires minor changes to an otherwise prosperous and contented life.

If you look back over your lifetime up to now, you notice that you are not the same person you were at a previous stage in your life. The adolescent is a different person than the infant, the young adult is a different person than the adolescent, the middle-aged adult is a different person than the young adult, and the senior adult is a different person than the middle-aged adult. You in a later stage of life think, act, and respond to life in a way significantly different from a previous stage of life. When you think, act, and respond to life differently than you did before, then you have effectively changed your experience of life, because how you think, act, and respond to life determines what you get and do not get in life, and achieve and do not achieve in life. It determines the quality and quantity of your relationship and connection with yourself and other people, which is the defining creative force behind your experience of life.

The natural changes that occur from one life stage to another mostly occur subconsciously, hidden from conscious awareness, requiring no conscious effort. The downside to this natural process of change is that we have no say in our experience of life; we simply get what life decides to give us, which may be far from what we truly want. Creating change using conscious awareness is a dramatically different process. It requires energy, commitment, will, suspension of credulity, humility, and open-mindedness. This is what makes what should be an easy and natural process seem insurmountable.

My goal in writing this book is to give the reader the understanding and means to effect significant and purposeful changes in his or her experience of life. The psychological concepts are defined and presented in a logical and detailed manner. The content is accompanied with examples from history and personal experience to help the reader gain the required understanding of the origins, evolution, and operation of the psychological concepts that drive the reader's own personal experience of life. More importantly, I give the reader a detailed methodology for successfully directing and implementing the desired changes to his or her life experience.

I include passages from the Judeo-Christian Bible to give clarity and credulity to the concepts explained in this book. This is not to evangelize any religion or religious denomination. The fact is that the Judeo-Christian Bible is still one of the best and most complete references for the understanding of the power of the human belief system and the requirements for consciously implementing changes that will significantly alter the experience of life.

Most of us have parts of ourselves that we hate and hide from the world and ourselves. This book helps the reader explore, discover, and make peace with all of himself or herself. It is when we can accept all of ourselves that we find wholeness, and it is in our wholeness that we find our perfection.

It is my sincere hope that many will be helped by the concepts and methodology provided in this book.

David Saffold
April 27, 2017
Nashville, TN USA

CHAPTER 1

The Great Law of the Universe–As You Believe, It Is Done unto You

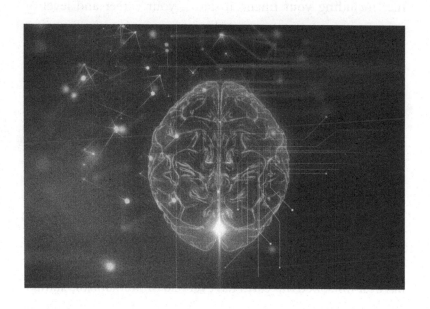

David J. Saffold

What Are Beliefs?

You are an incredibly powerful being! It doesn't matter if you believe this to be true about yourself; it is true nonetheless. You have the power of belief, and beliefs are what create your experience of life. More importantly, you have the power to change your beliefs, and this gives you the ability to change your experience of life. I mean every aspect of your life, including your financial status, your career and level of power and responsibility, your social status, your marriage and intimate relationships, the circles of friends and associates to which you belong and feel comfortable, your self-esteem and self-confidence, and the level of contentment and happiness you feel about your life and yourself—just about everything about your life. All these aspects of your life are dictated by your beliefs, and since you can change your beliefs, you have the power to create the experience of life that you choose.

Your beliefs give you the ability to see something that does not exist and bring it into existence. No other living creature that has ever inhabited this earth has ever had this remarkable ability. The proof is irrefutable. All you have to do is look around your environment. Your house, your car, your computer, your town, your country, and even the civilization of which you are a member were all, first, ideas in the minds of people. Every nonliving man-made thing you interact with in your daily life was first an idea, concept, or vision in someone's mind. The alphabet, writing, language, computer, desk, and the office in which I am writing this book all owe their existence in reality to a thought or idea in someone's mind. In fact, this very book you are reading started as an idea in my mind. Our beliefs take ideas and make them realities.

Your beliefs are not mere thoughts. Your beliefs create your thoughts and drive your actions and reactions to life's events. Beliefs are rooted in a deeper level of your psyche, extending beneath the layer of conscious thought and awareness. They are the motive force behind creative endeavor, both constructive and destructive. Your beliefs are not concerned about what is actual or real. Many of your beliefs are not actually true; you just believe they are, which makes all the difference when it comes to the experience of life that is your current reality. A simple example of this phenomenon is the first voyage of Christopher Columbus in 1492. He believed the world to be round, which is actual fact, and therefore he believed he could get to the lucrative trading ports of India by sailing west from Spain. However, many of his crew believed the earth was flat and that falling off the end of the earth was a real and terrifying possibility, which is not actual fact. Their belief in a flat earth almost caused the voyage to fail. Not only that, when they did make landing, they believed they were in India, which is why we still use the term Indians for what are actually Native Americans. If not for Columbus's beliefs, that voyage would never have occurred. It was his beliefs that enabled him to reach North America and be credited with changing the course of human history. Those who believed the earth to be flat had a different experience of life, and changing the course of human history by sailing to North America was not a part of that experience.

Your beliefs are the bundle of convictions, judgments, concepts, ideas, and definitions that you feel are absolutely true about yourself, other people, life, and the world. Your belief system's purpose is to help you survive in the physical world as well as the emotional world that drives human society and is mainly concerned with detecting threat in order to protect you from physical and emotional harm. Your beliefs fall into three main categories: personal or core beliefs, interpersonal or collective beliefs, and physical beliefs.

Physical Beliefs

Physical beliefs define the physical world in which you live and interact. They tell you what things in your physical environment are good for you and what things are harmful, and what is a threat and what is not a threat. For instance, you do not usually stick your finger in an electrical outlet because your belief system warns you of the harmful consequences of doing such a thing. Your physical beliefs are mostly concerned with helping you understand, interpret, and safely negotiate the physical world in which you interact.

Collective Beliefs

Your interpersonal or collective beliefs are those you share with other people. Collective beliefs are what create, define, and maintain human civilization and organization. The idea of nations, economies, governments, religions, and all the other institutions that enable and maintain collective human life and activity within the framework of human civilization is based on the collective beliefs you share with other people. For instance, your shared beliefs with the other people who are citizens of the United States of America are what give existence to the nation called the United States of America. Most citizens of the United States of America share common beliefs concerning the physical borders that define the physical part of the earth that collectively belongs to the group of people known as the United States of America. They also have common beliefs concerning the republican form of democratic government, the right of personal freedom, and such.

Why is it that you give someone a piece of paper and he or she will give you food, a house, a car, a weapon, or something tangible and of real value that is necessary to maintain your life? He or she can't eat that piece of paper you gave them in exchange for food. That piece of paper won't defend the person from his or her enemies. Try swinging a piece of paper at an enemy with a gun and see who wins that fight! It can't shelter the person from the elements or keep him or her warm in winter. Yes, we call that piece of paper money, but it is still just a piece of paper. Your collective beliefs enable you to exchange an object of no real value for something of definite real value. It is the common belief you share with other people that makes this so. You and the person who gives you the product or labor in exchange for the piece of paper share a common belief in the good faith and credit of the government of the United States of America. Because of this common belief, the person you gave that worthless piece of paper to believes that he or she can also exchange it for something of real value. People don't just think this but have a deep conviction that it is true. If they had any doubt that they could exchange that piece of paper for something of real value, they would definitely not give you something of real value in exchange. Neither would you!

Imagine that you want to sell your car and some stranger approaches you and writes on a piece of paper that he will give you something of equal value in the future if you give him your car right now. Would you give him your car? Surely not! You have no faith or trust that he will do as he says. But you do have the required faith and trust in the government of the United States. This faith and trust in the government of the United States is what gives value to those pieces of paper we call dollars. This faith and trust is a type of belief, and it is this shared belief that maintains our national economy. If you and enough of your fellow citizens lose faith or start to doubt the government's ability to back up its currency, our whole economy will collapse; this actually happens all the time. The collapse of the German economic system after World War I is a good example. The country of Venezuela is suffering from a collapsing economy in the present day.

Changes in our shared beliefs unleash huge amounts of energy. We give these periods in human history fancy names to denote dramatic changes in the collective belief system of large groups of people. The Renaissance, the French Revolution, the Industrial Revolution, the Scientific Revolution, the Dark Ages, etc., are all times in history where the collective beliefs of large groups of people underwent a dramatic shift.

The Renaissance is the period in human history where these collective beliefs transitioned from the superstition-riddled beliefs of medieval times to the new beliefs needed to drive the Scientific Revolution. These new beliefs led to the Industrial Revolution and the modern world we live in today. This is a good example of the incredible creative power that is unleashed by a constructive change in beliefs. When new beliefs arise in a few, human consciousness is set free to expand and encompass more possibilities for life, which propels creative action. As the new beliefs spread to more and more people, greater amounts of creative action are unleashed. This process proceeds exponentially. For instance, the standard of living of mankind has progressed more in the past couple of hundred years than in all previous history, all due to the changes in beliefs that accompanied the short period in human history called the Scientific Revolution.

The major religions of Christianity—Islam, Buddhism, and Hinduism—are other examples of the power that is unleashed by changes in the collective belief systems of large groups of people. A man called Jesus of Nazareth taught new beliefs to a small group of people. After a few hundred years, these beliefs had spread throughout the populations living around the Mediterranean basin, including ancient Greece and the peoples incorporated within the ancient Roman Empire. With the crumbling of the Roman Empire and the dissolution of the Hellenic civilization, it was the Christian beliefs that formed the foundation of the new Western civilization that emerged and in which we live today. The beliefs traceable to one man, Jesus of Nazareth, unleashed an incredible amount of energy over time, and we are still living in that energy. The same incredible amounts of energy were released by the beliefs that started with Mohammad and Siddhartha Gautama, the founders of Islam and Buddhism, respectively.

Beliefs can be destructive as well. Destructive beliefs within the collective consciousness of groups of people are the root causes of wars and destructive conflict. Nations that have let shame or a sense of inferiority (usually masked by projecting superiority) creep into their national belief system have produced the most destructive wars in human history. These destructive beliefs ultimately work to destroy the host, as was experienced by Germany and Japan in World War II. When a group within a larger group becomes a victim of these self-destructive beliefs, violent civil wars can erupt that wreak terrible destruction on a nation. The wars of religion that ripped apart Europe after the Reformation are another example of the carnage caused by destructive beliefs in groups of people.

Personal Core Beliefs

Your personal beliefs, or core beliefs, are what really count when it comes to your personal world and the life you experience. Your core beliefs are the beliefs you hold about yourself. They are what define your self-worth, self-esteem, self-confidence, and whether you are a good or a bad person, and how good or how bad you are. Your core beliefs also contain your basic definitions about other people and life in general. For instance, if you believe life is something to fear, then you will disengage from life as much as possible. On the other hand, if you believe that life is an exciting source of opportunity, then you will seek to maximize your engagement with life.

Your core beliefs determine everything about your personal life: the types of people you marry, the types of people you befriend, the types of jobs and careers in which you engage, and the general level of prosperity you experience, rich or poor or somewhere in between. Your core beliefs also play a major part in addictions and destructive behavior. They are usually the major culprit behind your failure to create the changes in your life that you truly desire. When you feel stuck in your experience of life in terms of the types of people you date and marry, how you are treated by other people, the amount of money you make, how you make your living, or anything else you don't like about your life, the cause usually lies within your personal core beliefs.

Most people feel that the flow of power comes from outside of themselves. This is true in the physical dimension of life because we live and interact with other beings and physical forces that can project power. At the level of your personal world, power actually flows from within you to create your outer world. The power and forces within you, your beliefs, create the life you experience within the realm of your personal world. It determines what you have and what you don't have in your life and the people with whom you associate and share intimacy. Everything about your life right now has been determined by how you have used and managed the power within yourself, the power of your beliefs.

Your beliefs determine how you interact with people, and your interactions with people determine your experience of life! How you respond to and interact with people determines much of what you get and don't get in life. Your financial income is determined by people. Your profits and losses in business are all about people. Your family life, romantic life, business and work life are all about people. Your social status, and popularity, or unpopularity, are all about people. Pretty much every aspect of your life that is really important to you is all about people. Thus, how you interact and relate to people is the vital component creating your experience of life.

How Beliefs Create Your Life

When you experience an event, it must be interpreted in order for you to take the appropriate action in response to the event. Your belief system is the event interpreter. One of its main jobs is to decide whether the event poses a threat to you either physically or emotionally. Your belief system takes in all the information surrounding the event and checks its store of historic information for seeming similarities between the current event and the experiences of past events stored in its historical archives. It uses this matching process to determine the impact the event will have on you, including the severity and imminence of the impact. In other words, your belief system makes a judgment call about what effect the event will have on you, the threat level of the effect, and the timeliness of the effect. Once interpreted, your belief system returns an emotional bundle of thoughts and feelings, and these thoughts and feelings drive the actions you take in response to the life events you experience.

Bible wisdom: "Give, and it will be given to you: good measure, pressed down, shaken together, and running over will be put into your bosom. For with the same measure that you use, it will be measured back to you" (Luke 6:38 NKJV).

The actions you take in response to an event create another event in your immediate world. The event your actions create triggers a response, or reaction, from that which your actions impinged. The reaction contains the energetic qualities and intensity of the emotional bundle that dictated your actions. This means that the response you receive from your actions will also contain the energetic qualities and intensity of the feelings and emotions that fueled your actions. Think about how you treat someone who does something nice or pleasant for you. You most likely respond in a nice and pleasant manner. Now think of how you respond to people you believe have hurt you or betrayed you. When you take action in response to events you experience, that action becomes an event for other people to experience. They, in turn, must respond by taking some type of action dictated by their personal core beliefs. Their response creates more events for more people, and on and on. The responses from life create your experience of life, and the responses from life that you receive are determined by the actions you take in response to the events you experience.

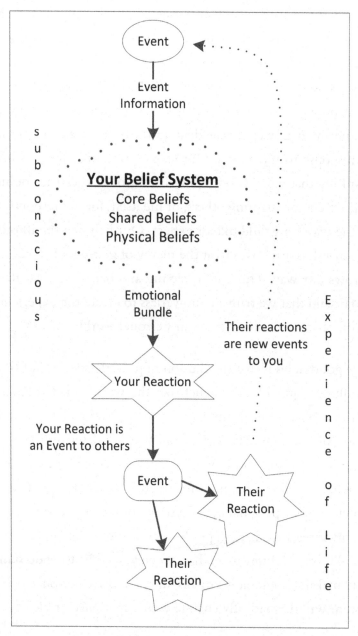

Figure 1.1. How your belief system creates your experience of life

All of these actions and reactions are happening below the level of conscious thought because our core beliefs mostly reside deep within our subconscious, creating the illusion of powerlessness. Our experience of life seems to be driven by hidden forces from outside of ourselves because we are unaware of the inner power that is driving the actions we are taking in response to life events. Our lack of awareness fools us into thinking that we are not responsible for our experience of life, and we end up blaming others, or life itself, for not responding in the way we would like or expect. Our belief in the illusion of powerlessness leaves us at the mercy of getting whatever life throws our way. This entails feeling and believing that life is unfair and that we truly are powerless to create the experience of life that we desire within our personal world.

The good news is that the illusion of powerlessness is just that, an illusion, just like the belief that the world is flat is just an illusion. Neither have any basis in reality. When you become aware of the core beliefs you hold that are determining your experience of life and how they can be changed, the illusion disappears, and you become empowered. When you create new beliefs in your personal belief system, an incredible amount of energy is released that can produce momentous changes in your life. The possibilities are endless when you come to understand that making some adjustments in your own personal belief system will dramatically change your experience of life.

How Beliefs Drive Your Reaction to Life

Let's look at how this all works by taking each element of the sequence in turn, starting with events. Physical events are the most common form of events. Physical events are events that you experience that happen in the physical world. Your physical senses of sight, hearing, touch, and smell are all sensors for detecting physical events. When you see something, hear a sound, smell an odor, or feel a texture, you have just experienced a physical event. You also have nonphysical sensors. An example of detecting an event using your nonphysical sensors is when you feel someone is looking at you, and you turn around to discover that someone really is looking at you. Imagine the myriad events that you experience every day, or just every hour! Anything that "happens" to you physically or psychologically is an event that you experience. An example of events is seeing a person, and hearing him or her saying something to you. When you have a conversation with someone, you experience a series of events as you see his or her facial expressions and body movements; hear the words the person is saying and the tone, pitch, and loudness of his or her voice; smell any smells emanating from him or her; see the type, color, and condition of his or her clothes; feel any physical contact that happens; and all the rest of what you see, hear, smell, and feel in a tactile manner. For our purposes, we will bundle this whole series of events you experience when talking to someone into a single event. Seeing the expressions and body language; hearing the words as well as the tone, pitch, and loudness of the voice;

his or her smell; and appearance are the event information embedded in the particular event. The event you experienced is having this particular conversation with this particular person on this particular date and time. Bundling all the myriad of events that we experience into a single event is how we talk about events in everyday speech. Keep in mind that the event has a beginning time and ending time, and that over this time duration you experience a whole host of events referred to as the event information. The event information associated with the event is a vital part of the interpretive step that comes after the event in the sequence.

Once the event happens, it is interpreted by your belief system in order for you to determine and make sense of what you are experiencing. You need to know how the event will affect you. Will it cause you physical or emotional harm and, if so, how much harm will it cause? Is the event something you want to happen? Will it make you feel good, or will it cause pain? Will it get you something you want, or will it get you something you don't want? One of the main jobs of your belief system is to protect you from experiencing pain or harm. To do this, it must determine the threat level the event poses. The threat level includes not only the severity of the harm the event might cause but also the immanence of the harm that will be caused. If you are riding in a car and see the car in front of you is getting closer, your belief system will respond with a warning signal. Because the car is relatively far away, the threat level is mild. You keep going as you were but also keep an eye on that threatening car. A little later, the car's brake lights are on, and it is decelerating quickly and getting close very fast. Your belief system takes this event into consideration and determines that the threat level is high, and you take immediate action to avoid crashing into that car. How does your belief system know that this car poses a threat to you? It knows because it has been taught. Its first lesson came when your parent yelled and violently yanked you back from the road when you were three or four years old. Then all the lessons that came thereafter about the dangers of crossing the street, looking both ways, and all the other frightening warnings you were taught by the media, teachers, and parents when you were young. You also probably heard many stories about people being killed or severely hurt in car crashes while growing up. You also might have experienced all the emotional terror of actually being in a car accident when young. All the experiences and emotions you have felt while driving in the past have been archived by your belief system. The fear that you felt and the circumstances surrounding that time you were almost hit by a truck when learning to drive, and all the other close calls you had while driving as well as the emotions and the intensity of the emotions you felt when experiencing those events, are logged by your belief system, which confirms the high threat level assigned to this type of event. Because your belief system was taught that being in a car crash can cause serious injury or death, it assigns a very high threat level to any event that resembles any of that historical event information in the archive. The terror and the intense emotions you experienced in the past associated with how a car crash will affect you are still there, deep within your belief system.

Your belief system also has an executive function. Once it has come up with an interpretation of what is happening, it needs a way to make you do something, take action of some sort. It does this by issuing a bundle of thoughts and feelings. In our example, you take action by hitting your brakes, or maybe even turning the steering wheel to swerve away from the car that is stopping in front of your car. Before, while you were driving along, you might have been feeling happy listening to some great song on the radio, or bored, or a little annoyed about something at work, or some other neutral or low intensity feeling. None of these thoughts and feelings would make you violently push the brake pedal and violently turn your car. But when your belief system perceives that the event information it is monitoring is highly threatening, it floods your mind and body with intense fear that results in the actions you take to avoid harm. Your adrenalin system is engaged, and you act quickly. After the threat is over and you are safe, you still feel your heart racing and the fear of what might have happened. You might also remember some of those past experiences where you had a close call or were actually in a car accident. You feel all those past emotions stored in your belief system.

Every event you experience must be interpreted and responded to with some form of action. An action can be either physical or nonphysical. Physical actions are when you physically do something: run from danger, hug someone, hit someone or something, go to a meeting at work, eat a meal, brush your teeth, say or yell something to or at someone, beep your car horn, purchase something, borrow money, ask someone for something, dig a hole, shoot a gun, pet your cat or dog, etc. Nonphysical, or psychological, actions are when your actions take place in thought. Instead of physically assaulting someone who has offended you personally, you just imagine assaulting him or her, or have thoughts that express anger and hate. Worrying and procrastination are forms of psychological actions, as well as fantasizing about doing something to or with someone or something in the future. Creative thinking, wherein you imagine new things or how to overcome challenges, is also a psychological action. It is important to understand that you respond to every event you experience in one form of action or another.

The actions you take involve a charge of energy. The action of fleeing from a hungry grizzly bear has a much greater energetic charge than clipping your fingernails. The intensity of the charge of energy is determined by your belief system. Your belief system has all the past emotional intensity archived along with all the event information from past event experiences. The emotional intensity is embedded in the threat level that the belief system has assigned to these types of events. When your belief system interprets a current event and its surrounding event information as something that is highly threatening, then it issues an emotional bundle with a very high intensity level so that you will react quickly and energetically.

The action you take in response to an event may take several paths depending on the interpretation of the event by your belief system. If the interpretation is that the event is safe and good, then your belief system issues an emotional bundle aligned with that experience, and you respond accordingly. For instance, someone does a nice thing for you or says something nice to you. This feels nice and pleasant as well as very safe, and you have thoughts of gratefulness and appreciation for that person. Your action in response to these types of thoughts and feelings is to say something nice and pleasant and act friendly and nonthreatening. The tone of your voice is mild and friendly, and your physical expressions and movements convey these feelings to the other person. But if you feel hurt or threatened by what that person said to you, then your response might be much more energetic and forceful. You might raise your voice or yell at that person as well as choose words designed to attack and hurt that person. Your expressions and movements will be more forceful and threatening.

Now imagine that you are sitting in your car waiting for the light to change when another car stops beside you in the other lane. You look over, and the person in that car smiles and waves at you. What are the thoughts and feelings you experience with this event? You might have thoughts of *What a nice person*, or *That's my nice neighbor*, and feelings of happiness and kindness.

These thoughts lead to the action of smiling and waving back to the person. Another thought pattern could be, *I don't know that person. Why is he or she waving at me?* and feelings of annoyance leading to actions of ignoring the person's greeting. What if you recognize the person as someone you don't like? You might have thoughts of, *What an idiot,* and feelings of anger leading to you shooting that person the bird. Notice how your reaction resembles the thoughts and feelings that are produced by your interpretation of the event you experienced.

Your actions are driven by your interpretation and the thoughts and feelings that interpretation returned, not by the event. What if the person you saw waving at you was a nasty neighbor of yours that you don't like, and you flip the person the bird and drive off in a huff? When you get home, the nice neighbor you do like comes up to you and asks why you flipped him or her the bird when he or she waved at you. Ah, something went wrong. You thought it was the nasty neighbor you don't like in the car, but it turns out that is was your nice neighbor. Your action was based on your interpretation, not the actual event. The important point to understand is that your interpretation of the event is what drives your actions, and your interpretation of events may or may not be related to the actual event. It is your belief system that interprets events, so it is ultimately your belief system that drives your actions and reactions to the events life presents to you. Your actions create the responses you get in life, and these responses to your actions determine your experience of life.

Most of your experience of life is directly related to your particular and unique personal belief system. Your belief system is what interprets the events in your personal world and creates the thoughts, feelings, and emotions that are your conscious life. These thoughts, feelings, and emotions drive your actions and reactions to life's events, which, in turn, determine how life responds back to you. Constructive beliefs lead to responses from life that enhance your life, while destructive beliefs lead to responses from life that are destructive to your life. Our destructive beliefs are the main cause of our failure to realize our life's ambitions and the life experience we truly desire.

The Origins and Development of Your Belief System

Most of our personal belief systems comes from outside of ourselves. It is taught to us starting the day we are born. Many factors go into the belief system we end up with as an adult. How deeply we feel emotions, predispositions to depression, and the like are inherited from generations past. Because of all these variables, people can have much of the same experiences in childhood yet end up with very diverse belief systems. For our purposes, what matters most is your unique personal belief system. Exploring and understanding the factors that created your belief system is helpful in understanding why your life experience is what it is, and, more importantly, the changes required in your beliefs in order to effect the changes you desire.

A Beginner's Guide to Perfection

When you were born, you had very little in terms of a belief system. You did have some that came to you through DNA, but most of what you need to survive in life was not yet created. You had to rely on your parents to survive. Your parents, or nurturers, are the ones who took care of all your basic needs. They protected you, fed you, kept you warm and safe, and nurtured you. You had some reflexes and could cry out when you felt discomfort, hunger, or cold. For the most part, however, you were a blank slate waiting to develop the belief system that would enable you to, one day, leave your parents and take on life for yourself.

You had no experience of the events of life, and that is what builds a belief system. Babies are born with incredible curiosity. They soak up every sound, touch, smell, and sight they experience. To the utter horror of their parents, they put just about everything their little hands grab into their mouths. I remember my three-year-old daughter smearing paint all over her face as she lapped it up like milk. They are experiencing things through their sense of taste, touch, and smell. This is how they build their physical belief system. Everything they see, touch, smell, and taste is being archived into their physical belief system. As they grow, they are able to experience more by going outside the house and exploring a bigger world. They discover that certain insects can hurt them, that concrete is hard and hurts when fallen upon, and the myriad other things that must be experienced in order to be able to survive in the physical world. All this is archived, rated, and cataloged in their physical belief systems.

Babies also start building their personal core beliefs. They soak up the emotional energy that pervades their environment. During their first few years of life, the emotional energy in their environment mainly comes from parents and siblings. The emotional energy associated with love, joy, happiness, anger, and sadness that is expressed in their environment along with the physical actions that accompanied these emotions is integrated into their belief systems. All this is archived, rated, judged, and cataloged. A baby or young child has not developed the emotional intelligence needed to understand that the emotions expressed by others are about the person expressing the emotions. Young children can only conclude that what they feel and experience from the impact of the emotions being expressed must be about them. When the baby or young child experiences nurturing emotions from others, then positive core beliefs develop. Experiencing repetitive loving attention over time helps a growing young child create positive core beliefs. On the flip side, continuously experiencing fear, anger, or neglect is conducive to producing destructive core beliefs. Destructive core beliefs cause most of our problems in adulthood. Because much of our core belief system is developed when very young, it gets submerged within the subconscious. By the time young adulthood arrives, our core beliefs are set and functioning beneath conscious awareness.

A Beginner's Guide to Perfection

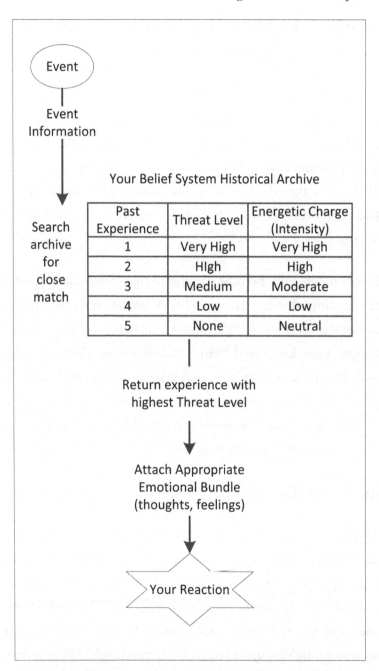

Figure 1.2. How your belief system processes events

David J. Saffold

Chapter 1   Important Concepts and Exercises

The important concept to understand from this chapter is that your beliefs are the ultimate power brokers in life, and you could not function or survive in this world without them. Your personal core beliefs are what create your experience of life because they define your relationship with yourself and are what determine your level of success or failure in every aspect of your life.

Before moving on, become convinced that your beliefs are what are creating your experience of life. If you are not certain, then reread the sections on "Personal Core Beliefs," "How Beliefs Create Your Life," and "How Beliefs Drive Your Reaction to Life." Relate your own experiences with the examples presented in this chapter to help you understand how your beliefs are driving the actions your take in response to the events you experience in your life.

Important Exercises:

Think of a memorable event in your life that happened recently: an argument with your spouse or another person, something that happened at work, or some other event of note. Write down a short description of what happened. What feelings did you experience? What produced those feelings? Did someone say something that upset you or made you laugh? What actions did you take when you felt these feelings? Did your feelings make you say or do something in response? What thoughts or judgments did you have when you felt those feelings? Notice the relationship between the feelings and what you did or didn't do.

Start becoming aware of the feelings that accompany the actions you take during a typical day. When something happens, analyze how you reacted and the feelings you felt that fueled your reaction. Record your analysis to help you begin to understand how your beliefs are creating your experience of life. Here are some examples.

This person said something that I felt was critical of me. I got angry and said this or that to that person or another person because I wanted to retaliate and cause the person harm. Or I felt hurt or hopeless, so I ate a gallon of ice cream that night, which led to feeling like a failure with my weight loss plan or in life.

My child failed a test at school. I felt fear, shame, or guilt because people might think I am a bad or inadequate parent. I angrily yelled at my child and said things that made my child feel ashamed, which made me feel even more like a bad and inadequate parent.

What kind of beliefs would produce the feelings and thoughts you had in response to the events you experienced in the above exercises?

David J. Saffold

What feelings and thoughts come up when you think of changing your life more toward what you want your life to be? What kind of core beliefs would produce these thoughts and feelings?

CHAPTER 2
Destructive Beliefs

Your core belief system contains both constructive and destructive beliefs. Constructive beliefs are beliefs you hold about yourself that are conducive to a life experience that is aligned with your true desires and that confirm healthy levels of self-esteem, self-confidence, and self-worth. For instance, beliefs that you are a success in life, a "good" person, worthy and deserving of good things, and that you have the ability to accomplish what you set out to accomplish, are all constructive beliefs. Destructive beliefs are beliefs you hold about yourself that create destruction in your life. They are beliefs that keep you stuck in a life not aligned with your true desires. The intensity and types of destructive beliefs you hold determine the intensity of the destruction that these beliefs wreak in your life. Milder intensities might keep you stuck in undesirable relationships, careers, or jobs, whereas highly intense destructive beliefs can lead to an extremely horrid existence, violence, and death.

Destructive core beliefs

Self-hatred is a generic term I use for destructive core beliefs because they define parts of a person that the person hates about himself or herself. People are very ashamed of these definitions of themselves and go to great lengths to hide them from others. Beliefs that you are evil or bad, a failure in life, unlovable, stupid, ugly, and the like are all self-hating destructive beliefs. We all have destructive core beliefs of one form or another that limit us in major or minor ways. Destructive beliefs seem to be inherent to the human experience. The doctrine of original sin and the biblical story of Adam and Eve's fall from grace are some examples of man's attempts to explain the inherency of destructive beliefs in humanity. The violence and abuse people perpetrate on themselves and others all stem from destructive beliefs within their core belief systems.

Have you ever thought that life is unfair? My children, when young, loved to proclaim that *it* is unfair! What they were really saying is that they were not getting what they wanted. I am the youngest of four children, and this was my mantra growing up. My older brothers got to go to bed later than me and see television shows and movies that I was not allowed to watch. It felt like I was always missing out on the fun stuff. It was so unfair! As a young adult, struggling with alcoholism, I looked out and saw people going to college, getting money, houses, cars, families, and all the things I wanted but could not have. It was like there were two worlds, I in one and they in the other. My world was for those who had nothing. Their world was for those who had it all. I had tried many times to make the crossing from my world to theirs, but the gulf separating these two worlds was impassable. I was stuck in a world I didn't want to be in, and life was unfair, very unfair.

Yet, here I am happier with my life than ever before. What happened? Was I miraculously healed of these beliefs that were causing such destruction in my life and preventing me from having the life I truly wanted to live? No true miracles occurred in the sense that we think of miracles. I found the answer because I really wanted to change my life. It took lots of hard work and time, but it was worth every penny I invested. Over the years, I have been able to change my beliefs to align more with the life I wanted to experience. As my beliefs changed about myself and my life, my outer world had to change to match my changed inner world. I came to understand that power flows from within to without, not from without to within.

Why do you get what you get and don't get what you don't get in life? How come, no matter how hard you try, you end up in the same place in life? How come you can't seem to improve your financial situation even though you try so hard and want to so much? Why are you stuck in a job or career that you don't like or want? Why do you always end up at the same dead end in your romantic relationships? Why is it that you want to change so much in your life but nothing changes, no matter what you do or how hard you try? Most of us are very perplexed about how unfair it all seems. Why do others seem to easily get what you want so much? If you really want to know the answers to these questions, then you have come to the right place. In fact, it is all pretty simple when you know how things work. It all starts with why you respond to life the way you do, because that determines your experience of life.

I know now that life will give to me much of that which I ask of it. But, when I was younger, I didn't know how to ask and sure didn't know how to receive. What seemed to come naturally to so many, I had to learn. Asking, accepting, and receiving are all about how you respond to life and what you give to life. How you respond and what you give is all about the thoughts and feelings you apply to life, and these ultimately emanate from the deeper beliefs and attitudes you hold about yourself and the world in which you live.

I worked many years in corporate America as a computer applications and database developer. I enjoyed automating manual operations and creating data systems and web applications. I got a big kick out of converting inefficient manual systems into automated web applications. I really liked the "wow" effect that I got when I did this. I also enjoyed the creative part of building these automated computer systems. This skill was a great selling point, and so I moved from job to job pretty often in order to get more money. My loyalty was to my talent and abilities, not to the company that employed me.

I had a bad concept of corporate America. I saw it as an inhuman machine that cared not for the people that fueled the engines. Many of its employees lived in fear of losing their livelihoods because the machine liked to spit people out for no apparent reason. I also saw the insanity of the power struggles, intense fear, and desperation that seemed to drive the people that called the shots in the companies where I worked. I really wanted to get out of corporate America and do my own thing, but I seemed stuck. How could I do what I really wanted and succeed financially? I felt energized going into these jobs and creating cool computer automation. I felt important when bosses and coworkers praised my accomplishments. When I attempted striking out on my own, my energy and motivation dissipated into thin air. I was terrified of going broke and losing everything and failing at life.

I remember working at a large corporation where I created a lot of great automation. They were very appreciative of the great things I had accomplished, which made me feel very important. After about a year, a new guy came in to help set up a formal project management system. He liked to tell me how he had been a bigwig in a lot of big companies and that he knew how to do everything under the sun. I smiled and waited for him to do something. I started seeing him meeting a lot with the department head. I saw them walking down the hall together schmoozing like they were old colleagues. Next thing I know, this guy is telling me what to do and how to do it. This infuriated me, and I began thinking of quitting and finding another job. My anger and frustration became so intense that I disconnected from the people in the department. I also started complaining in meetings about the sad state of affairs to which the organization of the department had sunk, and especially about our need for project management—about which the new guy had not yet done anything. I venomously gossiped about the new guy with a colleague that also felt the way I did. Eventually, my anger couldn't be contained and was

A Beginner's Guide to Perfection

displayed publicly when it boiled over in a group meeting he was leading.

I ended up getting a call from the director of the consulting firm through which I was hired. He said that the new guy had called him about my behavior; the new guy worked for the same consulting firm. My anger knew no bounds! How dare he tell on me like that! This is when I started feeding on the endless loop of all my anger and frustration. I felt powerless, and that increased my rage and fear. I started to fear I was losing my job. I actually had it pretty good: great pay, nice and respectful working environment, and pretty interesting work. I got to work from home when I wanted, which provided lots of freedom for a corporate job. My looping rage kept me up at night, and I barely slept for two nights straight. I was miserable, emotionally and physically. Something had to give, so I set up a meeting with my department head as well as the director of my consulting firm.

I talked to the director of my consulting firm a couple days later. I told him that I had a big problem with the new guy acting like he is my boss. He said the new guy had some praise for my abilities, and he wasn't just complaining about me. He asked me why I cared so much about what I worked on since the job of being a consultant or contract worker was to do whatever was asked of me. I explained that I didn't do manual processes because I was the automation guy; the new guy had tried to get me to take over a manual process. I told him it was very important for me to do great and important things at work. I felt annoyed with him because I felt he wasn't so much concerned about what I felt was important as about losing the contract. I wasn't too happy after talking with him, but I did calm down a little. I was starting to feel better, and the looping had gone from continuous to sporadic. I finally got a good night's sleep.

It occurred to me that I had a similar experience in past jobs. I would come in and create cool computer applications that brought me much praise and acclaim—the "wow" effect. Eventually things would start going downhill as the creative aspect of the job evolved into uncreative maintenance. There is no praise and acclaim for maintaining what is already built. I would start getting frustrated and angry; it would build, and finally I would have a blow-up and quit or get reprimanded and then quit; the same pattern at each job. I always told myself that I was best during the creative part, but would get disillusioned when that ended and the boring maintenance part of the job set in. That was the story I told myself about why this pattern seemed to always occur. Was that true? As I thought more deeply about it all, I had a revelation.

What was really happening was that I was not feeling important. That was why I was so enraged and frustrated. My belief system interpreted the events I experienced with this new guy as "I am not important anymore!" This interpretation happened early on when the new guy first showed up, and so every subsequent event I experienced took on the same interpretation. Once my belief system decided this is what was happening, I could only see confirmation of my interpretation in all the subsequent experiences; the great law of the universe was at work. The new guy walking down the hall with my department head was a confirmation of my relegation to unimportance. The new guy sending meeting invites to me about some project that needs attention was just another confirmation of my unimportance; everything he did seemed to be more proof that he had stolen my importance.

He had become a major threat to me because of two deeply held beliefs of mine. I needed to feel important, and I was terrified of financial loss. Fearing that I may lose my job and suffer financial loss was very threatening to my deeply held beliefs around not having enough money. At the deep level of my beliefs, my very life was threatened. This explains why I was experiencing the rage and fear, and why I was attacking the new guy with such vehemence.

My revelation expanded to show me that I was trying to get my feelings of importance from my jobs. I had a deep-set core belief that I was not important and was trying to heal that belief with something from outside of myself—jobs. I knew that I could not heal the inside with things from the outer world but was totally unaware that I was trying to do that very thing with my jobs. This showed me why I was doomed to keep repeating this pattern over and over. I kept hoping that, one day, my job would finally heal my destructive beliefs about my lack of importance and worth to the world and life. Like an addiction, I was hooked on my jobs to make me feel better about myself. And like all addictions, you become stuck with something that ultimately begins to destroy you. This is why I couldn't seem to escape working for corporate America and succeed at my ambition of working for myself.

The power of belief is immense! My beliefs around my lack of importance and financial insecurity were so deep and abiding that I could feel that my very life was threatened when they were triggered. I can look back with my current awareness and see how these destructive core beliefs have shaped my whole life in terms of what I have and what I don't have. They had a major impact on just about every aspect of my life up to now. They had a major influence on the jobs and companies for which I worked, the amount of money I made, why I got divorced, why I never knew what I wanted to do in life, why alcohol almost destroyed me, why I had to leave the United States Naval Academy, why I couldn't get through college until age thirty-four, and why I thought I was a miserable failure most of my life. The destruction these beliefs caused in my life is tremendous!

Why did I so desperately need to feel important? I must believe that I am not important, with a high level of intensity. We all need to feel important, but the intensity of my belief made it destructive. It was causing problems in my job and had wreaked so much destruction in so many aspects of my life. This revelation also brought back a memory pertaining to my need to feel important. When I was four or five years old, I remember attending some kind of party with lots of kids my own age. It must have been someone's birthday party. My older brother was entertaining the little kids by giving them rides on his shoulders. I remember feeling so special when I was riding on his shoulders as all the other kids were begging for a turn. Eventually, he gave in and lifted up another kid on his shoulders and paraded him around. I can remember how deeply "unimportant" I felt when my brother put me down and took another. This memory tells me that I had this belief from a very young age.

When I was around two years old, a calamity struck my family. My grandfather, my mother's cherished father, committed suicide by shooting himself with a shotgun. He did this in his home, so my grandmother found him and the bloody mess that a shotgun blast to the chest will create. He had been very successful in real estate and owned a lot of properties that he rented out to soldiers stationed at Fort Benning near Columbus, Georgia. It was 1966, and the Vietnam War was heating up and draining soldiers out of Fort Benning for service in Vietnam. His business suffered from the loss of renters, which triggered his fear of financial failure. He believed that financial death meant physical death and so acted on his belief. I can say this from experience because I also have this belief and almost committed suicide when I felt like I was facing financial death. It doesn't matter that my grandfather really wasn't facing financial death; it only matters that he believed he was facing financial death. The interpretation of the events he experienced as financial death was certain, and so he felt the horrible feeling of being doomed to real physical death. He sank down into major depression and finally ended his pain with a shotgun.

At the time, my brothers and I were living with our mother and father in Atlanta, Georgia, about a hundred miles northeast of Columbus. My grandmother had been the accountant of the business but was now so emotionally devastated that she couldn't function. My mother had to take my brothers and me and move in with my grandmother to help manage the business and sale of properties in order to save the financial situation around my grandparents' real estate business. My mother was also extremely traumatized by her father's suicide. I was two years old, and the world exploded around me. My mother was emotionally unavailable and emotionally unstable for years after this event. I am guessing that the little two-year-old became very unimportant to all concerned. The family trauma was so great that my mother and father ended up getting divorced a year or two later. That little two-year-old became even more unimportant. All my adult nurturers just vanished emotionally from my life. They could not give me much of the nurturing attention a two-year-old needs, and so I came to believe that I didn't mean much to anyone. I was not important.

Once that belief was set in that defenseless little two-year-old boy, it was all over. Each time I didn't get the attention that I wanted, my belief was verified and became more powerful. The trauma of being emotionally abandoned by my mother, father, grandmother, and grandfather—all the nurturers in my life—was so powerful that it set the belief that I was not important firmly into my belief system. Because I was so young, I didn't have the awareness or ability to mount a defense or question its veracity. My defenseless two-year-old mind could only conclude that I must not be very important because my grown-up nurturers (gods to a toddler) didn't pay much attention to me anymore.

Very young children cannot comprehend that their emotional pain is being caused by another. They can only conclude that they must be the cause of the emotional pain they are feeling. My immature and defenseless two-year-old mind needed to make sense of the emotional pain and trauma that was happening to him. The only thing I could come up with was that I must not be very important. I needed this to survive the years of neglect that followed due to the severe emotional suffering that plagued my adult nurturers.

I was way too young to verbalize this belief. At two or three years old, I didn't have the ability to consciously understand that I believed I was not important as I could when an adult. I could only feel the emotions and feelings of neglect and abandonment that went with the sudden change in parental behavior. I used to get so much loving attention, and now I got very little or none. Instead of loving kindness, Mommy is stressed and angry all the time, or doesn't come when I cry out. I am scared of Mommy and Daddy because they might yell at me if I ask for attention. All these experiences are going directly into my little two-year-old belief system.

The Origin and Development of Destructive Core Beliefs

When we were young children, we lived in a world of powerful giants. Our very lives depended on these giants. They fed us, sheltered us, loved us, tended to our needs, and they could also have killed us in a snap if they had chosen to do so. That's right, they had the physical size and strength to kill us or severely injure us at any time. They could also have chosen to stop feeding us, or sheltering us, or nurturing us. One of the built-in drives that nature endows us with at birth is self-preservation. We literally see our parents as god almighty, and God is all powerful, all knowing, the ultimate giver of life and death. God loves us, but there are consequences if God gets upset with us. A young child has a highly sensitive threat meter in order to survive in a world where he or she is weak and is easy prey for just about any other life form. This means that a young child is highly sensitive to the emotional energy of his or her environment.

Trauma is experiencing very threatening feelings and emotions that have an intense energetic charge. High intensity feelings and emotions can quickly create powerful and deep-seated beliefs. A powerful belief can be created by experiencing a single severely threatening event or a series of minor traumas. My grandmother and mother experienced a single severely threatening event with the suicide of a husband and father. That little two-year-old experienced a series of minor traumas over time. I was too young to comprehend what had happened to my grandfather. My experience was of the change in behavior of my parents, which lasted for years. I kept asking for the loving attention I needed and experiencing the inability of my parents to give me that attention. These repeated traumatic experiences of rejection built a powerful belief that I was not important to the world. As I grew older, I eventually stopped asking for or expecting the loving attention I needed to feel safe and important. It had become dangerous to expect something like that.

We get our most destructive beliefs when we are very young—ages zero to four or five years old. At this age, we are defenseless against the threatening emotions that are thrust into our psyches by those around us, including parents and siblings. We have not developed the ability to discriminate between our own pain and fear and that emanating from others. Our only logical choice is to conclude that "I am the cause of the emotional pain I am feeling, and, therefore, I must be the cause of my painful experience." A two- or three-year-old only knows that being rejected when needing loving attention must mean that he or she must not be important. These children can't understand that Mommy or Daddy is emotionally unavailable due to his or her own emotional problems and that the situation is not about their importance or unimportance, or about them at all.

The destructive beliefs that we develop at this young age are the most insidious because they go straight into our subconscious. We are way too young to have any conscious awareness of what is really happening to us. Our defenseless psychology only knows that "I am feeling these terrible feelings, and it must be about me." Because these beliefs are built subconsciously, they are free to grow in power unhindered and start directing our experience of life from an early age. By young adulthood, these destructive beliefs have hardened and become a major part of our personalities. They have become our truth and are determining our life experience.

These beliefs help us survive the emotional traumas of our youth. As a child, not being important helped me through the emotional pain of being neglected by my emotionally devastated parents. If I am not important, then I need not expect much loving attention from my nurturers. My belief made sense of my situation by convincing me that, since I am not important, it is normal and expected to experience the neglect and abandonment that I am experiencing. The emotionally traumatic and painful abnormality of the conditions I was living within was turned into the normality of my life, which, because of my belief, I could negotiate with a reduced amount of emotional pain.

Young children are not consciously aware of the beliefs they are forming to help them emotionally survive the first years of life. They only feel the emotional pain that the belief holds. Later in life, usually around the time of puberty, the belief will take on the "I Am" vocabulary. "I am a big Nothing!" "I am so stupid!" "I am a total failure!" "There is no way a person like that would have anything to do with a failure of a person like me." "I hate who I am!" "I am so ugly." "I can't do anything right!" ... the belief becomes an entity unto itself, as if it is another being that has a personality and consciousness. We literally have become our belief. It is our unquestioned truth about who we are and what we can expect from life. It is our god of gods and rules supreme. The saddest part of all is that none of it is actually true!

The normal experience for a child coming into human existence is necessarily emotionally traumatic. We come from a place of connected oneness into a worldly separateness, from within our mothers to outside of our mothers. This is emotionally and physically traumatic in itself. We then must experience the emotional separateness and trauma that exists in our nurturers, which heightens the emotional trauma in which we live and experience.

The intensity of the emotional pain, and the duration in which one lives in an environment permeated with traumatic emotional experiences, determines the power that the belief will hold over the life of a person. The more powerful the belief, the less chance that a more constructive competing belief can grow that will ameliorate the power of the destructive belief. If the destructive belief that is formed is very powerful due to intense and repeated emotional trauma at a young age, then that belief will prevent more constructive beliefs from forming. It will dominate the emotional life of its victim such that the victim thinks that he or she and the belief are one and the same. The belief will interpret all of life's experiences and events in terms of itself to help it grow in emotional power and dominance.

A Beginner's Guide to Perfection

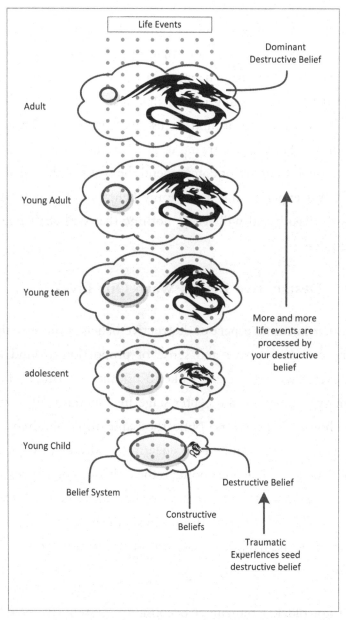

Figure 2.1. Growth of destructive belief in emotional power and dominance

The emotional pain I felt when my brother pulled me off his shoulders and picked up another for a ride was my belief telling me, "See, you really are not important, because, if you were, then this wouldn't have happened to you." This is what I felt even if I was too young to verbalize it mentally. My brother didn't stop riding me around on his shoulders because I was not important. He was just trying to give all the other eager little kids a turn. I could not comprehend the truth of the events of life I was experiencing because my belief was too powerful. It is the Truth and will accept nothing that will challenge its "rightness."

How Destructive Beliefs Warp Our Lives

Another insidious aspect of destructive beliefs is the way they warp our perspective and sense of proportion around the life events we experience. I like to use the cheering stadium analogy, where you are center stage in a stadium filled with ten thousand spectators. Nine thousand, nine hundred and ninety-nine love you and are cheering wildly in your praise. One is booing. The one booing is the only one you experience because it supports and proves your destructive belief that you are "bad." The 9,999 who think you are the greatest thing since sliced bread are irrelevant. This sounds pretty ridiculous, but it is how our beliefs really work.

As I got older, I remember becoming very sensitive to what I thought other people thought of me. If I thought someone thought "bad" of me, I would feel the same intense negative emotions that I felt when my brother stopped riding me around on his shoulders. I distinctly remember having this emotional sensitivity at an early age. When I was around ten years old, a classmate criticized my body by calling me a fatso. I was far from being fat but was not a skinny little kid anymore. This particular schoolmate and I had ended up alone in the school bathroom together and had some angry words. He had survived a house fire as a baby and was severely burned over much of his body so that his face and neck were grotesquely disfigured. In his anger, he called me a fatso. I don't remember much about the whole incident except for his criticism of my physical appearance. The irony is that here is a severely physically disfigured person criticizing another person's physical appearance. I was so emotionally devastated by this that I was starving myself, lifting weights, and running regularly by age twelve. A severely disfigured boy criticized my physical appearance, and I believed his words heart and soul to such a degree that I totally changed my life. My belief had grown in power and dominance. It was preventing the integration and formation of beliefs that would help me successfully negotiate life in the more complex and competitive social world of human interaction. I was literally stuck in the emotional world I had created when an adolescent surviving the emotionally painful environment of my family trauma. This is the nature of how these destructive beliefs work. They become cruel dictators tolerating no challenge to their dominance. They prevent us from creating more mature beliefs that help us succeed later in life and so leave us to contend in the more complex and sophisticated world of adult social life with the emotions of a devastated child.

My belief of not being important had begun to severely affect my perspective. It had started morphing into self-hatred. All the chaotic emotional dramas that we normally experience during our middle school and high school years were interpreted as major rejection and proof that I was not only unimportant but also generally unlikable. This self-hatred prevented me from connecting with others and stunted my ability to form close and intimate relationships. I could not let anyone get too close for fear that they would come to believe about me what I believed about myself. The fear of others discovering the "truth" of me was too terrifying to contemplate, so I went through life trying to be what I thought others would like me to be. I had to live a lie because I thought that being myself was to be something unacceptable to the world. I lived in fear and anxiety that others would discover that I was a terrible, unimportant, and unlovable person. Life, which is all about people, was terribly threatening. I was filling up with shame and fear such that normal consciousness became very painful. When life becomes threatening, there is no break from emotional pain. It is like being a blind man in a war zone where the threat of instant death can come from anywhere at any time. This made me a perfect candidate for alcohol and drug addiction.

When we feel threatened, our whole focus is drawn to the threat and surviving the threat. We necessarily are selfish in the sense that we are unable to take the feelings and needs of others into account. This has a profound impact on relationship building, which requires giving of ourselves and the ability to take another's needs into consideration and care. I was very threatened by life, and so my ability to care for the welfare of others was severely limited. This created trouble in the relationships I had and set me up for conflict and rejection, which further proved and exaggerated my self-hating beliefs. My beliefs were creating feelings that led to behaviors that were literally creating situations that led to the fulfillment of the belief.

Because life felt so threatening, I could not trust or form a sense of loyalty to a group of people from an early age. I played baseball and football starting in the peewee city leagues up through high school. I remember feeling no loyalty to any team for which I was a member. I just didn't care about the group, whether it won or lost, lived or died. I joined clubs in high school but didn't really participate. I just couldn't feel that I was a part of a group. I also remember feeling this way with my close group of friends in high school. I remember feeling that I was always a little less important to others in the group compared to how important I thought other members were to each other. I was always projecting my self-hatred onto others and believing what my beliefs were telling me about what they thought of me. They, of course, would sense this negative self-attitude and react to it, causing them to not really trust me and, in my mind, confirm my feeling that I wasn't really important. If I couldn't have confidence in myself, how could they? Every little imagined slight was further confirmation of my self-hating beliefs.

The constant stress and anxiety started affecting me physically as well. By my junior year in high school, I became prey to insomnia. I just could not fall asleep at night and would lie there all night long until time to get up and go to school. I also would have bouts of stomach pain and break out with small painful blisters all over the palms of my hands. The insomnia was so unbearable that I started drinking a glass full of my parents' vodka to get to sleep. I had discovered the relief that alcohol gave me from my anxiety and depression around this time, so using alcohol to help with my insomnia was a logical next step.

I was sixteen years old when I became addicted to alcohol. It gave me the release from the constant fear and anxiety I felt all the time. I could talk to pretty girls and be at ease with people. Alcohol acted as a euphoric for me instead of a depressant. The euphoric way alcohol affected me and my self-hating destructive belief system was the perfect combination for addiction. The intensity of my addiction to alcohol quickly progressed, and it was not long before it was causing trouble. I was able to keep the drinking to mostly weekends during high school, so my grades stayed good enough to help me get an appointment to the US Naval Academy. This had been my ambition in high school. I was going to go to the Naval Academy and become a hotshot fighter pilot and then a famous astronaut. If I could do all this, I would finally be healed of my unimportance. I would finally be somebody important, somebody lovable. I would finally get into the kingdom of heaven! My belief had come to so dominate my life that it was all I lived for or thought about.

I lasted almost two years at the US Naval Academy. My addiction to alcohol created so much trouble that I felt compelled to leave in the middle of my second year. I had a tendency to drink to the point of blackout or unconsciousness. The Naval Academy only let you on the town from noon to midnight on most Saturdays; the rest of the week, we were confined to the academy grounds. This helped me keep my grades decent and me out of trouble except on Saturdays. I started racking up trouble because I would get drunk and end up breaking some rule or another concerning our behavior when away from the academy. One Sunday morning, I was called into the company commander's office and confronted with a complaint from a naval officer who said I acted disrespectful toward him during a group trip to a football game at another college. I didn't remember a thing. I had gotten so drunk that I blacked out. The problem was that when I blacked out I didn't act intoxicated, but seemed pretty normal. This is an example of the type of trouble I seemed to create. Anyway, the summer after my first year, I was stopped for DUI while driving on Fort Benning. This incident was reported directly to the Naval Academy, which frowned very seriously on their midshipmen driving drunk.

This was a very serious infraction, and I was made to pay by being confined to academy grounds pretty much indefinitely during my second year. My anxiety, insomnia, and depression had not abated, and the weekend drinking was the only relief I found, and it was now gone indefinitely. This was more than I could bear. After trying to hold on, I finally gave in and requested to leave. I had talked to my parents about leaving, and they had agreed that they would help me get into a college when I got home.

Leaving the Naval Academy was a huge blow to my quest for importance. I felt like a giant failure now that I had lost all the honors and accolades that had gone along with such an achievement. My bucket of shame had risen to the full mark. I convinced myself that I could become great and important somehow by attending Auburn University in Auburn, Alabama. I would become an engineer and invent ingenious things, get rich, and make it into the kingdom of heaven that way. The next few years were really me drinking more, dropping out of colleges, failing, running away, and trying to start over and continue my road to success and the kingdom of heaven. Eventually, I ended up jobless and living with my parents. I couldn't support myself and had to rely on my parents.

I had become worse than nothing! I couldn't even support myself as was expected of a grown man. I remember how my shame and sense of failure talked to me. It would say "I am the biggest piece of junk God ever created." Anything I tried to accomplish to help myself get out of my lowly situation always ended in failure. I thought I was somehow defective because I couldn't do what I saw others easily doing, like holding a job, having relationships, making it in life. My destructive beliefs had become god almighty for me. My whole being was my "unimportance," my nothingness. I really was defective and the biggest piece of junk God ever created. I lived with the horrid pain of my shame as long as I could. Eventually my doom seemed too much to handle, and I started thinking of the only way out that seemed plausible—death. I didn't truly want to die; I just wanted the terrible pain to stop. Suicide had become the only option to stop the pain since everything else I had tried ended in failure and worse pain. The way I was going made it only a matter of time before I would have to check out for good.

My parents finally had enough and made me leave. I simply went across town and moved in with my grandmother. She was lonely and welcomed me with open arms. The pain of my life continued on unabated. One night I took my revolver and put it to my head at half-cock. I was drunk, so I don't know how I didn't end up shooting myself immediately. I sat there with the gun at my head trying to get the courage to touch the trigger and fire the gun.

Attending Alcoholics Anonymous had not cured me, but it had introduced me to a deeper idea of God. I didn't understand what it all meant, but I wanted to. I didn't know how to surrender my life to some God I didn't know and could not see. Suddenly, a thought took over my mind that said, "Your best thinking has gotten you drunk with a pistol at your head." I thought about this ... all the best thinking I could muster had led to living off my grandmother, drunk, and about to shoot myself. It was like I was looking into a cosmic mirror that enabled me to see the truth for the first time. My thinking was the problem! It was what had led me into the horror in which I lived! This was the first time I ever saw reality. It was the first time I saw anything without the filter of my destructive beliefs. I was twenty-five years old and never drank again. The next day, I left my grandmother's house. A few years later, I was married, a college graduate, and was earning a decent living. I was succeeding at life.

What happened that night to create such a change in my life? What happened is that I began the process of challenging my faith in my destructive beliefs and started creating new beliefs that conformed to the life I desired. As my new beliefs grew, the old beliefs lost their dominance and ability to create the experiences of my life. The new beliefs only needed a tiny foothold in my psychology to start changing my life in very big ways. As my new beliefs grew in power, I had more choices in life about what I got and what I didn't get, who I wanted to be with and who I didn't want to be with, and what I did and what I didn't do. More importantly, my new beliefs changed the way I responded to life. With this ability to choose, I had more power to direct my life and accomplish my desires and ambitions.

Before we move on, I want to recap the birth and growth of a destructive belief using the example provided in this chapter. I want to point out that our destructive beliefs come from the outside and are not an original part of our true selves. They were created within us when we had no defense or choice about accepting or rejecting them as a definition of who we are. At first, they help us survive the emotional pain of our environment when we are too small and helpless to defend ourselves in life. They become destructive when they grow to dominate and prevent us from transitioning to a new set of beliefs necessary to succeed in the adult world.

1. My grandfather committed suicide, which created emotional trauma in my parents.
2. The emotional pain suffered by my parents altered their behavior in a way that created a destructive belief in me that I was unimportant, at an age where this belief entered directly into my subconscious mind.
3. My parent's change in behavior lasted years, which allowed my destructive belief to grow in power and become my way of surviving the emotionally painful environment in which I lived.
4. My destructive belief warped my perception and sense of proportion such that I would credit experiences that

seemed to prove my belief and ignore or discredit the multitude of experiences that proved otherwise.

5. When I reached my teenage years, my destructive belief had transitioned into multiple forms of generalized self-hatred that became the dominant beliefs I held about myself.
6. My destructive beliefs caused me to fear that others would think of me like I thought of me. This created chronic fear and mistrust of people and an inability to form intimate relationships or honest and meaningful connections with other people. The fear of people led to missed opportunities in life and feelings of isolation that further proved my self-hating beliefs.
7. My chronic fear made me try to be what I thought others wanted me to be in order to feel likable and important to them, which led to conflict, rejection, and failure. This also proved that I was what I believed.
8. The emotional pain induced by my self-hating beliefs led me into a destructive addiction to alcohol.
9. My addiction to alcohol caused me to do things that created more shame and further proved my negative beliefs about who I am.
10. Eventually, my life became totally consumed by my destructive beliefs, and I ended up losing all that I valued in life.
11. As I believed it had been done unto me!

A Beginner's Guide to Perfection

Mine is an extreme case where my self-hating beliefs became so powerful and dominant that they almost killed me. The severity of my case is not uncommon, and many are done to death by their self-hating beliefs every year. The deaths ascribed to suicide as well as drug and alcohol addiction are most likely cases where destructive, self-hating beliefs became so dominant in their victims that they killed them. A more usual case is where these beliefs are present to a lesser degree such that we are prevented from growing to our full potential. Our ambitions are thwarted, and we stay mired in a life where we are always longing for something better. Our ambitions around intimate relationships, creative expression, money, and everything else seem to be up against an impenetrable barrier that keeps us stuck. Maybe we don't dare have ambitions, thinking that what we have is all we deserve. There are so many ways these beliefs filter and warp our perception of reality and what is possible in our lives.

Another way these destructive beliefs warp our lives is how they keep us stuck in the merry-go-round of seeking resolution in outer things. Our whole life becomes a quest to show the world that we are not what our destructive beliefs tell us. If I can just make a lot of money, get that man or woman, that car, that house, that outer thing, then I will finally be what I don't believe I am right now. Even when we get some or all of whatever thing we think will cure us, we find that we still need something more to finally get the job done. Outer things do not change these destructive beliefs. They are just too much a part of our core definition of ourselves. The cure must come from within.

Destructive Voices

Our beliefs have an uncanny ability to learn from our experiences. As I got older and experienced more of life, my belief in my lack of importance incorporated these new experiences and situations into its lexicon. It added a voice to its collection of emotions and feelings. This voice is very perfectly conducive for gradually increasing its power and control over our lives. Now it can tell you how unimportant you are, or how bad or ugly or disgusting you are. Now it can tell you how big a failure you are in life or how hopeless it is to want something better in your life. It can tell you that if you try, you will fail, and how awful that will be. It combines its words with fear, hopelessness, and the whole host of painful feelings and emotions in its arsenal to prevent you from believing something, and thus doing something, not according to its mandates. It is like our beliefs have become a conscious being unto themselves, separate from us, yet an integral part of our being. We are possessed by "demons."

When I was around forty years old, my first wife and I divorced. About a year or so afterward, I started dating, mostly through internet dating sites. I noticed that when I viewed profiles of women that were physically attractive to me and seemed confident and successful in life, I would shy away from contacting them and asking to meet. Having noticed this behavior, I looked deeper into myself and waited for the feelings to trigger and discover what was happening. Sure enough, while looking at a promising profile on the dating site, I heard the voice. This voice told me, "That woman will never want you because you don't make enough money." Along with the voice came feelings of fear and rejection, and the highly threatening chance of having this woman think I was an unimportant nothing. Wow, no wonder I would shy away from contacting and dating the women that were most attractive to me. Because I was aware of the concepts I am writing about in this book, I had the ability to challenge the voice. When it fired off its words, I answered it with the wisdom that "I don't want to be with a woman that only wants me for my money." I will never forget the vision of seeing the little gremlin that said this to me huff in frustration at not having me believe its words. It angrily smirked and disappeared.

The sad part of this story about my dating adventures with this destructive voice is that I believed it for most of my life up till my late thirties. Before I came to have some power and choice over my beliefs, this destructive voice of criticism, low self-esteem, fear, and failure was the words of God for me. I believed them as the gospel truth and reacted accordingly. Looking back, I now see that I abandoned so many wonderful opportunities because the voice prevented me from simply reaching out and grasping them in hand.

I liken these beliefs to an actual destructive being, much like the classic description of Satan. They seem to have intelligence and consciousness. How did my demon know to use the money trick to prevent me from contacting women I was truly attracted to on the dating site? It somehow knew that I was most vulnerable to the money trick because it knew I had beliefs that lots of money was the measure of success and attractiveness. It knew that I had powerful beliefs that if I could just become wealthy I would finally be attractive and lovable to the world. It knew about these beliefs and used them to do its bidding and keep its power over my life. This ability to play on your most threatening beliefs is the essence of its power over you. How did it acquire this ability to so completely trick me and keep me under its control?

I don't really believe in demons or that we are really being possessed by the minions of Satan. The reality is that our self-hating beliefs have incorporated the voices, feelings, and events that we have experienced over our lifetimes. Every experience we had where we believed we were bad, ugly, stupid, a failure, a nobody, unimportant, naughty, sinful, selfish, or any other adjective that fit our self-hating beliefs, was incorporated into our belief system along with the negative feelings and emotions and surrounding sensory information that we experienced during that event. Every time you were told by parents, teachers, siblings, or anyone else that could impact your life that you were bad or ugly or stupid, that event was logged into your belief system. By the time we reach adulthood, our belief system has a myriad of past experiences from which to draw and apply to a current event.

One of the main functions of our belief system is to keep us out of threatening situations. When you contemplate an action, your belief system, like a computer, searches its database of past experiences for anything remotely similar to the contemplated action or behavior that contains a hint of threat. It then orders these seemingly similar past events in terms of the most highly threatening, and those are the ones it brings into your conscious mind along with the voices, feelings, and emotions that are stored within those past experiences. Our belief system is simply trying to protect us from threatening situations. Like a computer, it is simply pulling up information that tells us that if you do this, then this horrible thing will happen according to previous similar experiences in its stored archive of data.

The problem is that a bug has become embedded in our threat detection program. This bug is a destructive belief that has gotten stuck in our belief system during the early stages of its development in the form of an infinite positive feedback loop. As we grow older and experience more disparate life events, our threat data archive comes to be flooded with threat data associated with life events that are, in reality, innocuous, or even positive or good for us.

When that little boy's brother put him down and picked up another little boy for a ride on his shoulders, he logged this event as threatening because he interpreted the event as proof that he was not important. In reality, this event was not a threat but simply my brother giving the other children a turn to ride on his shoulders. But the little boy's belief system couldn't tell the difference because of the programming mishap that had occurred when his threat detection program was first being developed. His warped belief system interpreted this event as a threat and logged it as such in his data archive. This results in it being more likely that subsequent life experiences that are, in reality, nonthreatening will trigger a false threat signal and be logged as another threatening event. Like a snowball rolling downhill, the progression increases geometrically. Because of this infinite positive feedback loop stuck in our threat detection system, by the time we reach adulthood, much of life feels painfully threatening.

If you came out of childhood with very powerful and dominant destructive beliefs, like I did, then your belief system is full of highly threatening experiences that apply to just about everything in life. This means that when you contemplate taking actions that will move you toward something in life you desire, you are instantly filled with fear, doubt, indecision, and lack of confidence. Your belief system has filled your conscious mind with a host of highly threatening past experiences, and the feelings, emotions, and voices connected with those experiences are stored therein. This painful array is way too pervasive and powerful for your unaware and unaided conscious mind to handle, and so you give up your contemplated actions as a lost cause, making even a positive effort much more difficult. This precipitates another round of feelings of self-disparagement and hopelessness that proves the veracity of the destructive belief. The destructive belief literally gets to say to you, "See, I told you this would happen if you tried to do that!" This is why we stay stuck in current situations that we want so much to change. This is why we will stay in situations that are, or have become, very harmful. They seem safe compared to the threat that our beliefs tell us are the consequence of trying to change.

I remember when I first heard my destructive voices as something separate from myself. I had recently purchased my first mobile phone and set up an account with a mobile phone carrier. This was after my divorce when I was living on my own in a small apartment. I had been growing in my awareness of the ideas in this book at the time and so had been asking my "Inner Helper" to help me hear the voices that went along with what I would feel when my destructive beliefs were triggered. The concept of an "Inner Helper" is explained in the following chapters. Anyway, one day, I decided to go to my mobile phone carrier's website and check how many minutes I had used that month. This was before all the carriers offered unlimited talk and text, and so I was charged an arm and a leg for any monthly overages. When my phone bill popped up, I discovered I had gone over my allotted minutes, and my phone bill for the month had ballooned from something like $40 to more than $200. That's when it hit! I remember hearing voices calling me things I wouldn't call my worst enemies. "You are such an *idiot*!", "You are so irresponsible!", "What a loser and a failure you are!" My prayers had been answered, and I heard the destructive voices that were attached to the feelings and emotions that I experienced when my destructive beliefs were in action.

Later, when I analyzed the voices I had heard, I noticed that some had come from other people who had been angry at me for some reason. This experience showed me why I felt the horrible emotional pain that went along with my beliefs. Imagine what it feels like to have someone very intimate with you call you an idiot, or stupid, or irresponsible, or a failure in life. That is what I called myself for making a $200 mistake. It's not just the words that are used, but the tone is violent, angry, and very shaming. Whatever is saying these terrible things to me really believes them with all its heart and is very upset and angry with me.

When you are under the power of your destructive beliefs, you are usually not aware of the voice because you have no objectivity. You and your beliefs have become so integrated that you experience them as your true self, not the separate emotional energy that they really are. When they define you as stupid, incompetent, irresponsible, ugly, gross, a hopeless failure, an idiot, weak, or defective, you experience the painful feelings and emotions that anyone would naturally feel when believing such things about himself or herself. They keep you a child in a grown-up world, powerless.

In the following chapters, I will discuss in more detail how to mitigate the effects of these destructive voices. Now is a good time to get in touch with your own voices. Take some time to investigate some of the self-critical mantras that you tell yourself. Write down the exact wording. What are the self-critical words you hear about yourself in the different situations in your life? What are the critical things you tell yourself about your status and abilities in your job and career? What about your abilities as a parent, spouse, or intimate partner? What about your financial status and physical appearance? What about how you think other people think of you?

You don't just hear the voices; you feel the voices as well. It is very important to become aware of the emotional and physical feelings that accompany the voices. These feelings are signals that let you know which of your destructive beliefs are active. For instance, you may feel like you have a knot or weight in your solar plexus, the center of your chest, or in your throat. It might feel like a general depressive malaise where you feel sluggish and de-energized. Anxiety in the lower stomach or chest area is another common feeling. I sometimes get a sensation in my forehead and around the top of my head that feels like those areas of my brain have shut down. I have learned that these feelings flare up when I am emotionally overwhelmed. As you become more familiar with your voices and the emotional and physical feelings that accompany them, you become more empowered to choose what action you should take when life events happen instead of reacting to the dictates of your destructive belief. When you have choices, your life changes accordingly. Below are some examples of the destructive voices that others regularly tell themselves.

The author of this book:

- I am a nothing.
- I am not important to people.
- You are the biggest piece of junk God ever created.
- You are such an *idiot*.
- You are so irresponsible.
- You are a failure at life.
- Look how fat and ugly you are.
- You look so disgusting.

A thirteen-year-old girl:

- I am an evil person.
- I am going to "perdition."
- I am a terrible daughter.
- I am not good at anything.
- I am ugly.

A twenty-something-year-old man:

- I am a total loser.
- I am worthless.

- You know everyone is just pretending to like you: everyone really hates you.
- You are a weakling, not a man.

A thirty-something-year-old woman:

- You are always going to be different and not good enough.
- I am just too sensitive for this world.
- Oh no, I look hideous; I am getting cellulite.

A forty-something-year-old woman:

- People are nice to me because they are being polite.
- I don't know what I am doing.
- If they really knew me, they would not like me.
- Most people are less anxious than me.
- I am really not that smart.

A fifty-something-year old man:

- I am a loser because I waste time.
- By this age I should have accomplished much more.
- I am a fool because I didn't do this twenty years ago.
- I am ugly and not attractive.

A fifty-something-year-old woman:

- You are selfish; think of something besides yourself.
- I am a bad mother.

- I am incompetent (about my work and career).
- It's just not fair; life is unfair.
- I am not lovable.
- He doesn't want me.

A fifty-something-year-old woman:

- I don't think anyone would mind if I wasn't here anymore.
- I am just a mess and people must be getting tired of me.
- I am getting fat.
- This (emotional or physical pain) is never going to end; it's going to go on forever.

A sixty-something-year-old woman:

- It's totally awful! (usually sung to the melody of "My Dog Has Fleas").
- I can't do this.
- I feel (am) unsafe.
- I feel (am) unwelcome.
- I don't fit in.

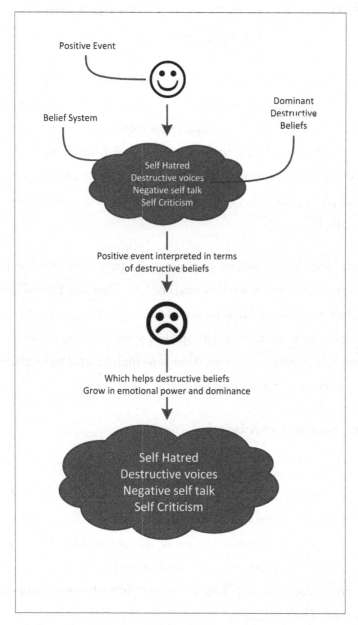

Figure 2.2. Destructive beliefs change positive life events into negative for their own purposes.

Chapter 2   Important Concepts and Exercises

The important concept to understand from this chapter is that your destructive beliefs warp your perspective of life and are the reason why you stay stuck in an experience of life you do not want. Your belief in their negative definition of yourself gives them the power to dominate and control your experience of life. They are what say no to the changes you want to make in your life.

Your destructive beliefs originated to help you survive the emotional pain of your first years of life. They are buried deep within your subconscious and have operated unabated and unchallenged over the entire span of your life. Over time they were able to add a self-critical voice to their arsenal to help keep you under their power and control.

Important Exercises

It is very important to become consciously aware of the destructive beliefs that are driving your experience of life. Start pulling them out of their hiding places into the light of your awareness. Become aware of the destructive voices you hear. Look over the examples of destructive voices at the end of this chapter to help you get in touch with your particular phrases of self-criticism.

Common scenarios seem more likely to bring on our destructive voices, such as when we make a big mistake of some sort, feel like we have hurt someone, or feel we have been hurt by someone, don't get what we expect, or something happens contrary to what we were hoping would happen. Try to be aware when you experience these painful events and write down the words of self-criticism that come up.

Ask a trusted friend to make you aware of self-critical phrases you use when talking about yourself or your life. They can hear what you can't.

CHAPTER 3
Your Personal World

Before we move on to techniques for changing our beliefs, we need to understand a little bit about the dimensions that make up our personal world. We humans each have our own unique personal world in which we operate and experience our lives. Our personal world has three main dimensions: the physical dimension, the emotional dimension, and the spiritual dimension. The physical dimension is where we experience the objects, forces, and energies that make up the physical universe. The emotional dimension is the home of our belief system. It is where we interpret our experiences and define how we respond to life. The spiritual dimension is where we know we are an integral part of the universe.

The Physical Dimension

We call the collective physical dimension the natural world, which includes all the forces, energies, and physical objects that make up the physical universe. Other life forms, man-made objects, planets, galaxies, earthquakes, tornadoes, radiation, gravity, matter, atoms, electrons, etc., are all examples of phenomena in the physical dimension. Our physical bodies and all the organic structures that make up our physical bodies reside within and are an integral part of the collective physical dimension. We are physical beings, which means there is no escape from the physical dimension. Like it or not, our physical beings are always in the physical dimension.

The things that exist in the physical dimension are temporary. Observation and experience show us that the physical universe is constantly re-creating itself. The things we know that are contained within the physical universe are created, exist, and destroyed—birth, life, death. The only constant seems to be the universe itself. Our physical bodies mimic the physical universe in that our cells are always re-creating themselves. They are created, live, and die. The cells that make up our physical body lead temporary existences compared to the lifetime of our physical body.

The physical dimension is a dimension of disconnected separateness. We see ourselves as separate from other physical objects in the physical universe. There is a "me" and a "you," a "me" and an "it," and "me" is separate and disconnected from "you" or "it." There is space between "me" and "you" and "it." Separateness gives the experience of boundaries and limits. I begin here and end there, whereas you begin over there and our limits are separated by an expanse of space. Our experience of disconnected separation in the physical dimension leads us to conclude that we are different from everything else in the physical universe. Difference is what allows us to feel threatened, because if you are different and disconnected from me, then I don't know you, and not knowing is threatening to me.

In the physical dimension, there is only one reality—the present moment. There is no such thing as past or future. Past and future are just concepts based on our experience of the present. Past is just our memory of an event that has already occurred. Future is an expectation, wish, hope, or projection of an event that we want or do not want to occur. Memories are our interpretation of events we have experienced and therefore are created by our belief system. This means that memories are distorted aspects of the events we have experienced. It is very common for two different people who have witnessed the same event to give different accounts of what happened. This is because each has interpreted the event according to their personal belief system. The point to get about memories is that they are our interpretations of events that we have experienced and may not have any basis in the actual reality of the event we are remembering.

Let's say you decide to walk down the street. The only thing you can truly know for sure is the exact moment you are in right now. The first step you take is really an infinite series of "now" events. Imagine all the tiny movements your body must make associated with the simple act of taking one little step. You raise one foot, move that foot forward a certain amount, then lower that foot until it touches the ground, then shift your weight and start the same process with your other foot. When you start this step you only have an expectation that you will end up being a couple of feet down the street at the end of the movement, but this expectation has no reality in the physical dimension.

Each infinitesimal event in the series of events that happen during just that one step can turn out to be something totally different than what you expect. An example could be that as you are lifting your foot up, a blood vessel bursts in your brain, and you fall dead to the ground. Or, let's say, something splats on your arm so you stop the act of stepping to look at what hit your arm and see bird poop all over your elbow. You took that step with the certainty that you would end up a few feet down the street, but the reality is something different than what you expected. This is what I mean when I say that the present moment is the only thing that has existence in the physical dimension. Events we have already experienced are just distorted interpretations, and future events are expected events that have not happened and may not happen at all.

It is very important for our purposes to understand that past and future have no reality in the dimension where physical life events occur. This means that, despite what we think or expect, future events are totally unknown. When it comes to what will happen, we know absolutely nothing. We may want this or that future event to happen or not want it to happen, expect it to happen or not expect it to happen, but the reality is that, to us, it is totally unknown. Not knowing is painfully terrifying for most humans. We humans really hate not knowing; we hate it so much that we will invent stories that make us feel that we do know! Then we will fight with those who have made up stories different than ours because their stories threaten our belief in our own knowingness. Our only options to avoid conflict are to convince, cajole, or force them into believing our story or to believe their story and concede that our story was wrong, that we really didn't know. Admitting that we don't know and will never know is usually too painful to consider.

Bible wisdom: "... that you may be sons of your Father in heaven; for He makes His sun rise on the evil and on the good, and sends rain on the just and on the unjust" (Matthew 5:45).

In the physical dimension, there are no good and bad or right and wrong events. The physical dimension makes no judgments of the events that occur therein. The judgments of events in the physical dimension are man-made inventions that we use to qualify our experiences of events. In the physical dimension, events are neutral; they just are. Reality in the physical dimension boils down to just "is." It just "is."

Let's say an earthquake strikes a large city and kills a thousand people. We say a bad thing happened and feel sadness and compassion for the victims and survivors of the earthquake. But the physical universe doesn't judge the event at all. The earthquake happened because of the pressures generated by the movement of tectonic plates within the earth. This same area of earth has experienced many earthquakes over the eons. This particular earthquake is just a normal event in the physical universe. The judgments we apply to events in the physical dimension are generated by our belief system and are entirely subjective. How do we really know that the earthquake that killed a thousand people is a bad or awful thing? If it did not occur at that particular place at that particular time, the whole universe might have collapsed or exploded, wiping out all life in the entire universe! Now the earthquake has become a good thing. Our physical death is also a neutral event to the collective physical dimension. When we die, the physical universe does not judge the event as good or bad. Our physical death is just a normal event in the physical dimension, just as our birth and life are normal, neutral events in the physical dimension.

The collective physical dimension is the place of ordered cause and effect. Every time this happens, that will happen. This is the basis of physical science and the theories and laws that seem to govern the actions we observe in the physical universe. The small slice of the physical universe that we have experienced is the physical dimension of our personal world. This is the dimension where we have dominion over things, where we give, receive, create, destroy, take, lose, hurt, break, possess, and own things. Property, houses, cars, people, our physical bodies, the earth's atmosphere, lakes, oceans, money, animals, etc., are all things in the physical universe under our dominion.

Your Emotional Dimension

Your emotional dimension contains your conscious thoughts, memories and expectations, beliefs, and emotions, as well as your subconscious beliefs, emotions, memories and expectations. It is the home of your belief system, including both constructive and destructive beliefs. Just like your physical dimension, your emotional dimension has sensors that we call emotional feelings. Your emotional feelings include sadness, happiness, peacefulness, pain, boredom, excitement, confidence, depression, etc. These emotional feelings let you know which emotion is active in your emotional dimension. Emotional pain, like physical pain, signals that your emotional body has sustained injury.

Unlike the physical dimension where existence is temporary, things that exist in the emotional dimension are indelible. Our emotional dimension permanently retains our experiences in the form of memories, which are actually our interpreted experience of past events. Every event we have experienced has been interpreted by our belief system and archived in our emotional dimension.

In your emotional dimension, you experience disconnected separation as well as past and future. Like in the physical dimension, we see ourselves as separate from other physical objects in the physical universe; however, in our emotional dimension, we experience past and future events. In fact, much of our conscious thought dwells in the past and future. We are constantly creating stories of future events based on our interpreted experience of past events. This helps us avoid the fear of not knowing what will happen next. One interesting aspect of human nature is that we can actually prefer to know that something bad will happen in the future over not knowing at all, even though not knowing must include the possibility that something good will happen instead. We are always being surprised by what actually happens compared to what we thought would happen.

Your emotional dimension is also where duality exists in the form of moral opposites, good or bad, right or wrong, fair or unfair, threatening or nonthreatening, etc. It is in your emotional dimension that you attach judgments and interpretations to physical events to create your experience of physical events. It is easy to understand this when you consider that someone else may judge that same physical event as good or right while you judge it as bad or wrong. This divergence of judgment between individual people is so common that we even have a figure of speech to convey this concept: "One man's meat is another man's poison."

Your emotions emanate from your belief system to produce the emotional feelings, or energy, that drive the actions you take with your physical body. It not only creates events in your physical dimension but, more importantly, it determines your experience of events encountered in the physical dimension. Think of it this way, when you were a baby, your physical body could do very little. As you grew physically, your emotional dimension gained experiences that grew your belief system, which enabled you to do more things with your physical body. You were born with an immature physical dimension as well as an immature emotional dimension. One thing that comes built into your innate emotional dimension is curiosity. This curiosity in your emotional dimensions drives our physical body to explore the physical surroundings so your emotional dimension can gain the cause-and-effect experiences needed to do more things with your physical body. Imagine the chaos that would result from your physical body growing up to adulthood without any growth of your emotional dimension. You would blabber like a baby and only be able to scream and cry to communicate your basic needs. You would be a danger to yourself and others because your physical strength would be operating without the experienced and trained operator it needs to appropriately negotiate the cause-and-effect reality of the physical universe.

Your Spiritual Dimension

Your physical body is really just earth formed into human shape. It is made of the substance of our planet earth. You sustain your physical body by eating plants and animals that are made of earth. All the constituents that make up your organic physical body are of the same substance as is the planet Earth. The planet Earth is made from the substances of our universe. Therefore, your physical body is literally formed from the same substances as is the universe. There is something in you that knows that you are integrally connected with everything in the universe. This knowing is what I call your spiritual dimension.

In the spiritual dimension, there is no separation, no past and future, and no good and bad or right and wrong, no fear or ecstasy. We are one with everything else in the universe, and all is peaceful. In this dimension, we are not disconnected and do not experience fear and threat because our belief systems do not function here. The spiritual dimension transcends the emotional and physical dimensions.

If you have ever been awed by the immensity of a starlit night, then you have flitted in and out of your spiritual dimension. Here is where you have sensed how ridiculously unimportant is most of the minutia you find yourself worrying about day in and day out. Being in our spiritual dimension is when we are taken to the mountaintop and can see reality instead of what our beliefs feed us. We are not fooled as when under the dictates of the beliefs that underlie our emotional dimension. In fact, our spiritual dimension is where we can observe our beliefs with clarity and understanding.

The energies of your spiritual dimension are more subtle than those of your emotional and physical dimensions. It takes a lot of practice to be able to consciously dwell in your spiritual dimension. Usually, we get there by accident once in every great while, if ever, when we find ourselves being still, and something shoves us over the top for a quick peek.

The spiritual dimension is the source of everything needed to maximize our life potentials because it is our connection to the immense power and energy of the universe. Yet, we spend the least time in this dimension because of the amount of conscious effort required. By contrast, chaotically bumping around in the physical and emotional dimensions requires relatively little conscious effort. It is so easy to run on autopilot, which automatically interprets life events from existing data of past experiences stored in our belief system to react to whatever life throws our way.

Consider the universe in its entirety as a unified whole. What can we say about it? It contains all of creation. It wields immense power and has unlimited energy. It is constantly renewing itself and creating things, all kinds of things. It does what it does perfectly and reliably. To sum up, it is all-powerful and everywhere and can be completely trusted to do what it does with perfection. If we put it in human terms, we would say that the universe has complete confidence in itself, is completely trustworthy, completely reliable, all powerful, and everywhere. Furthermore, if it is the creator of all things, then it must be all-knowing. What can be known that it doesn't know? Another wonderful thing about the universe is that it judges not. It doesn't care one way or another what you did or didn't do in the past or what you will do or not do in the future. It doesn't care if you are guilty or not guilty and never will care. It doesn't see you as bad and never has or will see you as bad or evil. It doesn't judge anything, anytime, or anywhere. It only and always sees you for what you truly are, its creation, its child, nothing more and nothing less.

How your dimensions interact to create life's opportunities

Bible wisdom: 'For whoever has, to him more will be given, and he will have abundance; but whoever does not have, even what he has will be taken away from him" (Matthew 13:12).

To prepare you for the next chapter in which you will start creating new beliefs I want to talk a bit further about the dimensions that make up your personal world. The Physical Dimension is the source of all the real events that you encounter. Your reaction to these physical events are produced in your emotional dimension. Your reaction has a significant influence on the future events that you will encounter. For instance, let's say you are very interested in buying a new car you recently saw advertised. You have always loved that particular model car and would very much love to finally own one. However, the price in the advertisement is somewhat higher that what you feel you can afford. How you react to the car advertisement will determine the future experiences you will have. To understand how your reaction to physical events influence your future, we will look at several different responses you could have to the experience of seeing the car advertisement.

One response might be that you would love to have that car but you know you could never afford it. Even if you could scrape together enough money to buy it, you would have to live in abject poverty for the rest of your life because you would be living from paycheck to paycheck. You don't feel secure in your current job and surely don't believe you could ever earn the money needed to ever comfortably afford that car. You have resigned yourself to driving the old car you currently have that breaks down just about every time you drive it. "Who am I to think that I could have a nice new car like that?" This response leads to taking no action in response to the car advertisement. Your car breaks down on the way to work the next morning and you are fired for being late again.

Or, your response could be the opposite. You really want that car! Not only that, you deserve a great new car like that and you know you will find a way to afford it. Sure, your job doesn't pay well but you are confident that you will continue to develop your skills and earn more money in the future. You trust that life will always get you through with flying colors. You are excited about all the great possibilities waiting out there for you. Your confidence and enthusiasm cause you to stop at the car dealership first thing the next morning and talk with the salesperson. You tell the salesperson that he or she might as well give you the keys to that car because you know it is already yours. You are so excited about that car that you get the salesperson excited for you. The deal doesn't work out right then because they still will not sell the car for the price you know you could realistically afford. You walk away disappointed, but not undaunted. Over the next few days you call several more car dealerships that carry that model car, but still have no luck getting the price down to what you can reasonably afford. You feel a bit discouraged and end up forgetting about the whole thing. A month later, the salesperson calls and tells you that the factory has significantly reduced the price on that particular model car because it is very overstocked. The salesperson says that he or she would be happy to sell it to you for what you had initially offered. You smile and go get your nice new car.

In our example, the first physical event you experienced was seeing the car advertisement. The two distinct reactions to this event were produced by your belief system in your emotional dimension. In the first response your belief system interpreted the act of buying the new car as threatening to your life. Your negative reaction led to taking no action towards purchasing the new car. It determined that your future would be like your present experience of life – driving an unreliable car and earning the same amount of money at a job you don't like. In fact, your reaction contributed to the loss of your job and the real possibility that you would descend into abject poverty – just like you believed.

Your other response was quite different and led to a significantly different experience of the future. Your reaction to the car advertisement was positive, energetic, and enthusiastic. Your belief system interpreted the advertisement as a great opportunity. This reaction motivated you to stop by the car dealership and have the conversation with the salesperson. Thus, your reaction created another physical event that included another person – the salesperson. Your excitement was contagious which motivated the salesperson to network with other salespeople about getting you that car for the price you could afford. When the salesperson discovered the price reduction, you were the first person he or she called. Your reaction to the first event you encountered, the car advertisement, led directly to you owning the car that you wanted. Your beliefs created a new experience in your future aligned with the experience of life you desired.

The important thing to see in this example is the direct correlation between the first event and the last event. Your reaction to the first event produced all the subsequent events you encountered in the chain. Even though the price was out of your reach when you first talked to the salesperson, you still got the call later on that got you that car. The crucial part turns out to be your initial reaction to the first event: seeing the car advertisement. It was this reaction produced by your belief system in your emotional dimension that created the opportunity for you to encounter the physical event of getting a call from the salesperson telling you the price had changed to something you can afford. This is how your beliefs create your experience of life. This is how your beliefs create the future events you encounter in the physical world. This is how your beliefs determine what you have and what you don't have, who you marry or don't marry, what you do for a living or don't do for a living, and how much money you make or don't make.

Of course, there are myriad possibilities that can happen. Even though you were very excited and talked to the car salesperson you might still have not ended up getting that car. The important point is that your reaction is dependent on your beliefs and greatly influences the future events that come your way. Another way to say this is that your beliefs attract to you those future events that correlate to your beliefs. Your beliefs are creating the opportunities that you have and will have in your life. It is not luck but your beliefs that are determining whether you are a "have" or a "have not".

When you reacted with enthusiasm, excitement, and motivation, your reaction compelled you to create a thread of opportunities in the universe. Talking with the car salesperson ignited a series of events of which you were never aware. The car salesperson contacted other salespeople in an effort to find a way to get you that car for the price you could afford. The opportunity you ignited kept spreading as the salespeople contacted others in their networks. Your beliefs were sending tentacles of opportunity out into the universe searching for that car at that price. This is how the physical and emotional dimensions interact with the spiritual dimension. Your emotional dimension determines your reactions to the physical events you encounter in the physical dimension. The reaction produced by your emotional dimension creates expanding threads of opportunities in the universe (spiritual dimension) that seek to return to you what your beliefs are expressing – "as you believe it is done unto you."

Our simple example is about buying a car but the same process is true for the more important facets of your life. Your job, career, relationships, financial level, and physical and emotional health all depend on the opportunities your beliefs are creating in the universe.

My wife and I decided to investigate what it would take to own our dream house. Our current house had appreciated somewhat over the years but we still owed a hefty mortgage. The perfect scenario was to sell our house and buy or build our dream house for a price that eliminated the need for a mortgage. We wanted to stay in the same general location which was currently highly priced. However, some areas in our zip code were faring better than others in terms of being a buyer's market. My wife searched for houses while I searched for land to build on. The architect I engaged was skeptical about building what we wanted for the price we wanted to pay in order to end up with no mortgage. During our conversation, I mentioned something about my long-standing interest in finding ways to build for less and how I had investigated using cellular concrete many years ago. Next thing I know, the architect gets excited and starts talking about a company that had developed a building method using preformed concrete panels. The gist was that using these panels would significantly lower the cost of building relative to the traditional way to build a house. At the time of writing, I don't know if the numbers will work out in order for us to move into our dream house with no mortgage. I still need to find out if using this concrete panel system is feasible for our purposes. My ambition and enthusiasm have ignited a chain of events and created opportunities yet to be realized. They are out there in the universe working on my desires and creating that debt-free dream house in my future.

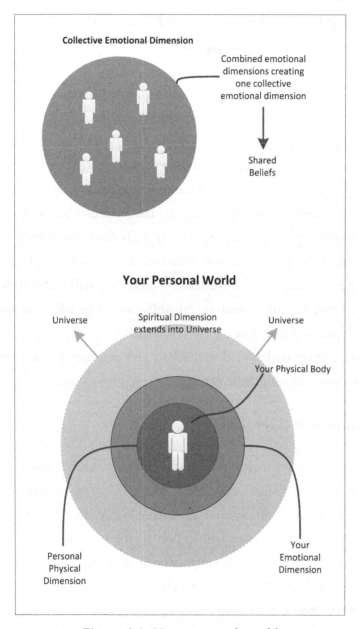

Figure 3.1. Your personal world

Chapter 3   Important Concepts and Exercises

The important concept to understand from this chapter is that your belief system lives in your emotional dimension, where it can operate in past, present, and future. This means that your beliefs not only interpret and define your current experiences but also define your memories of past experiences and tell you what experience you will have in the future. This ability to define your past and future gives it immense power over the direction of your life! For instance, if your beliefs interpret past experiences as painful failure, then they will tell you that the desired changes you are planning for your life will only lead to painful failure. This will mark your future plans as threatening, which will make you feel and act in ways that sabotage realizing those plans.

Important Exercises

Your spiritual dimension is your connection to the power you will need to change your beliefs. It is the key to your success. Reread the section on your spiritual dimension. Contemplate the logic proving your connection to the immense power of the universe—your ultimate creator and parent. Use your imagination to float around in the universe greeting all your siblings: hello, sun; hello, moon; hello, galaxy. Fly into an exploding supernova and feel the incredible power and energy of that event supercharging every cell of your body. Contemplate the incredible power, beauty, immensity, and perfection of the universe.

CHAPTER 4

Accessing Your Personal Power

Changing Your Beliefs

Two major changes are needed in your emotional dimension to create the changes in your life that you desire. One is to create and empower new beliefs that are aligned with the life you desire, and the second is to retract your faith in your existing destructive beliefs. In the previous chapter, it was shown that we all have the ability to do both. It is vital that your new beliefs counteract and begin to replace your faith in your destructive beliefs. There is no mystery about this process, which is quite logical. You are changing your beliefs by creating new beliefs that will replace old beliefs. Not only do you have this ability but you have done it many times in your life. Compare your current beliefs to those of ten years past. As you grew from toddler to young adult, many beliefs changed.

We naturally change our beliefs as we transition from one stage of life to another. The big difference is that the natural changes in our beliefs occur subconsciously and without any conscious intent on our part. In other words, we have no conscious choice in what we get in life and must take whatever life decides to give us. Now we are consciously choosing to change our beliefs by choosing the beliefs we want to create as well as the beliefs we want to let go. Remember that your life (physical dimension) is the effect of your belief system within your emotional dimension. You cannot create changes in your life without first changing that which causes the circumstances and experiences of your life.

Bible wisdom: "The Kingdom of God does not come with observation; nor will they say 'see here!' or 'see there!' For indeed, the Kingdom of God is within you" (Luke 17:20–21).

*Note: This Bible teaching states definitely that God and the kingdom of God are not found in the physical dimension. They are not actual places in the physical universe! Implicitly, we can also state that the kingdom of hell is also found within us and is not some physical place under the earth. Why the belief still prevails that heaven and hell are actual places in the physical universe and their rulers, God and Satan, are physical beings is a mystery.

In Chapter 2 ("Destructive Beliefs") I explained how our destructive beliefs have coalesced into a separate entity with consciousness separate from our own. Your most powerful destructive beliefs formed in your core personal beliefs when you were young. They formed in your subconscious out of range of your conscious awareness. They have spent all this time dictating and creating life experiences that maximized their power and dominance in your belief system. They also have been able to synergistically coalesce all the disparate ways these destructive beliefs expressed themselves in your experiences into a single entity, a personal Satan, if you will. This means that your destructive beliefs have integrated themselves such that they work together to maximize their power and dominance over your life. When they strike, you believe they are you, and that the experience they are feeding you is totally real.

Consider Earth orbiting around the sun. Its orbit determines the energy and radiation that it receives from the sun, which determines the conditions on Earth that support life. The ideal orbit creates the best conditions to enable life to flourish. If Earth's orbit is dislocated a tiny amount either closer or farther from the sun, then the conditions on Earth that support life would change drastically. The Earth's climate will become much hotter or colder depending on the orbital change that occurred. The severe climate changes will make life harder to sustain. Life will become more restrictive and threatening or even be snuffed out altogether.

In this analogy, think of you as Earth and your belief system as your orbit. The power of your destructive beliefs has dislocated your orbit from the optimal path such that life has become restrictive and much more threatening. What you need is to change your orbit back to its optimal position so that your life can flourish. Imagine the immense energy and force that is required to move a planet even a tiny amount! Moving a planet is an easy task for the universe; it does it all the time. In fact, it does much bigger things all the time! The universe has the required power needed to change your beliefs.

Creating Your Personal God

The first step in the process of creating new beliefs is to do just what our destructive beliefs have done by creating an entity in our emotional dimension that will contain, coalesce, and synergize the new core beliefs we need to create. We need serious help if we are going to successfully challenge the power of our destructive beliefs. To be successful, we need a reliable and trustworthy source of immense power and energy that will give us the courage, endurance, confidence, and wisdom needed to retake our emotional dimension and deflate the dominance of our destructive beliefs. We find the source of power needed by connecting to the universe through our spiritual dimension. The end point of our connection to the universe is the entity we create in our emotional dimension. This entity will synergistically manage and correctly allocate all the power and energy flowing down from the universe through our spiritual dimension into the new core beliefs we need to create. It will also have the power and ability to successfully challenge the power and dominance of our destructive beliefs.

Bible wisdom: "God is spirit, and those who worship Him must worship in spirit and truth" (John 4:24).

The entity that we need to create in the emotional dimension of our personal world is a personal God. I use the word *God* because this word represents unconditional love, omniscience, unlimited power, total perfection and goodness, and ability to do anything and make anything happen. In our and in all past and present cultures and civilizations, the word *God* represented unlimited everything. Therefore, it is a word that holds a great amount of power in the collective human belief system. I am not using this word in the religious sense or promoting a belief in the definition of the God of any religion. In fact, if you need to change the term to something else, then feel free to do so. Others have replaced the term *God* with terms such as "Higher Self," "Higher Power," "Ideal Self," "True Self," "Universal Goodness," "Universal Power," "The Force" (from *Star Wars*), etc. However, choosing some phrase other than *God* may not hold enough credibility for many, which may sabotage this process. It is vital that our new belief entity has the qualities and attributes that will do for us what we need done. In this book, I use the word *God* to represent the new belief entity we are creating.

This is the hardest part of this life-changing process because you come up to this point with a belief system full of doubt, threat, and all kinds of preconceived and hardened concepts of what is being asked of you in this step. The whole book up to now was written to prove to you that you can do this if you really want to change your life. All you need to do is to perform the experiment and analyze the results while keeping as open and objective an attitude as you can muster.

Defining Your Relationship with Your Personal God

Now that you have created a new belief entity or container called your personal God in your emotional dimension, you need to define the qualities and attributes of your personal God that align with the new beliefs you desire to create. Let's use the wisdom from the Bible to create the general attributes and qualities of the personal God of your personal world that you want to create.

Bible wisdom: "If a child asks for bread from any parent among you, will they give the child a stone? Or if the child asks for a fish, will the parent give the child a serpent instead of a fish? Or if the child asks for an egg, will the parent give the child a scorpion? If you then, being evil (having destructive beliefs), know how to give good gifts to your children, how much more will your heavenly Parent (your personal God) give the holy spirit (power to change your life) to those that ask their heavenly Parent" (Luke 11:11)!

This is one of the most profound teachings in the Bible because it gives us everything we need to create our personal God. It tells us what God's will is for us, how God loves us, what God is willing to do for us, and how God will help us do whatever we need done. It says that God relates to us as we relate to our own children.

If you don't have a child, then imagine if you did and ask yourself these questions:

- What is my will for my child's life? What do I want for my child's life?
- How much do I love my child?
- How willing am I to do anything in my power to help my child when my child is in need?
- Here is how I answer these questions:

- My will for my child is that he/she prospers in all aspects of his/her life, including relationships, career, finances, everything! I want only good things for my child.
- I love my child unconditionally. There is nothing my child can do that will cause me to not love my child as much as I always have.
- If my child is in danger or truly in need of something, I will do everything and anything in my power to help my child.

This is how I really feel about my own children. I have answered honestly about my love and will for my children. Now, why would I not want to create my personal God as a loving parent just as I am a loving parent but without the evil (destructive beliefs)? Here are the qualities and attributes of my personal God:

- God loves me absolutely, unconditionally, and eternally. Nothing I have done or will do can change God's absolute love for me.
- God's will for my life is all good. God never wants bad things to happen to me just as I never want bad things to happen to my own children. God's will for me is to prosper in every aspect of my life. This includes my relationships, career and work, money and finances, my emotional life, physical life, and my spiritual life. God wants only good things for me.

- My personal God is all powerful, much more powerful than my destructive beliefs. The immense power of the universe is wielded by my personal God.
- I can trust my personal God absolutely. God will always lead me rightly.
- My personal God always gives me what I need when I ask.
- My personal God knows and always tells me the Truth. God never lies to me or tries to trick or deceive me.

If I had the power to create God, this is the God I would create for myself. Wouldn't you create such a God? Now you have everything you need to create your personal God in your emotional dimension. Answer the questions that I listed. Write them down using your own words. Let yourself use powerful adjectives to add feeling and meaning. For instance, "I love my child" is very different than "I love my child with all my heart and soul!" and "I want good things for my child's life" is different than "I want incredibly great things for my child's life!" Do you feel the difference?

Many people feel that it is selfish to want good things for themselves. The word selfish means "sinful" or "evil" in our cultural belief system. We are taught, from birth, that it is sinful or evil to want things for our lives. This is a destructive belief in itself. It is natural to want things for ourselves. Our ambitions and creative desires are a natural part of our humanity. All of life is imbued with an ambition to grow to its fullest extent and glory. Should the oak tree feel shame for wanting to grow tall and strong? If nature imbues all of life with the ambition to grow to be all that it can be, then would not our personal God want the same for us? In fact, it would not be a stretch to say that our ambitions and desires for our lives are our personal God's ambitions and desires for our lives as well. They are one and the same!

Right now, you are simply being a scientist and setting up the experiment I am proposing. Don't let your doubt or judgments interfere with doing the experiment correctly. You are simply doing what I did in order to test the results for yourself. Give yourself the freedom to create your personal God with all the attributes and qualities you truly desire. Let yourself think of this as merely an interesting exercise to see how you would define *God* for yourself. Try to keep your own personal inhibitions out of the process by telling yourself this is just a creative exercise. Go all out with no holds barred. Imagine that some great creator of all existence chose you to represent it to all peoples on earth. You are instructed by this mighty creator of all existence to define *God* for all the peoples of Earth. The instructions further state that you get one chance, and what you come up with will be for all eternity.

Overcoming Resistance to Creating New Beliefs

One method for testing your defining statements for inhibitions is to ask yourself, "Is this what I would want for my own child or someone or something I love dearly? Do my statements convey the feelings I want them to convey? Or do they sound full of doubt and fear?" Allow yourself to rise above your destructive beliefs as best you can while creating your personal God. You may feel uncomfortable stating something like, "God loves me unconditionally," because you don't feel that you deserve to be loved unconditionally. These are the kinds of inhibitions you want to keep out of the process.

You may be tempted to think that creating your personal God is a silly thing that defies your credulity, like a child's imaginary friend. Actually, you are coalescing very powerful forces that lie deep within your spiritual dimension into a single integrated whole. Your destructive beliefs have effectively prevented you from synergizing these powerful forces, effectively leaving them scattered, dormant, and neglected. These powerful forces, which you already possess, can create powerful changes in your personal life. Furthermore, these forces are what have created all the momentous, world-changing events in human history. They are very real and very powerful!

If you are having a difficult time with the concepts and exercises presented in this chapter, then look back at your list of destructive voices from the previous chapter. You have believed in them and given them reality. Why? Aren't they just an imaginary devil? Why give all your trust and faith to this imaginary devil? Why can you believe in a personal Satan and can't believe in a personal God? If you can choose what you want to believe, then isn't it silly and foolish to choose an imaginary devil that loathes you over a personal God that knows you to be everything that is good and wonderful?

When I was twenty-five years old sitting there in my grandmother's house drunk and seriously contemplating suicide, something profound happened in my personal world. A new belief in God sprang up in my emotional dimension. It was not an earth-shattering, lightning strike religious conversion, but something a little less dramatic. Something deep within me shifted into a powerful decision to let the idea of *God* set up shop in my emotional dimension. I made a committed decision to do this experiment and see what happened—exactly what I am suggesting that you do.

I had read about using *God* in the literature of Alcoholics Anonymous and heard others talk about it at meetings I had attended, but it had made little impression on me. I really had no detailed instructions on what to do or how to use this new belief. I had some vague ideas about what *God* was supposed to be, such as all powerful and such, but I also had a lot of bad concepts and powerful doubts about the popular and religious concepts of God. In essence, all I had to go on was the little I had learned from Alcoholics Anonymous, my scanty religious training, and concepts and anecdotes from popular culture.

I thought very little about God. I did believe that there was a first cause or creator of all things, but this God or first cause didn't really have anything to do with me personally. Pretty much the sum total of my thoughts about *God* was that there must be a God or something that created the infinite universe we live in, but my only contact with whatever did create this universe will be when I die. I didn't have any clue, or much care about, how this God that I did not understand interacted with me personally.

Yet, this small beginning had the effect of freeing me from my addiction to alcohol. That was a huge change in my life, a change I had desperately wanted for many years but could not achieve with my old belief system. The impossible had become possible! My experience proved that minor changes in my belief system could produce giant changes in my life. But effecting this change in my life was not as simple as creating a new belief in my emotional dimension. I had to nurture and grow that belief. I had to keep feeding it larger doses of my faith and reliance. I had to grow my belief in its reality and power in my personal world. I had to feel confident that I could trust and rely on my personal God. I had to have proof that it truly was God as I had defined God and not just my destructive beliefs in disguise, a "wolf in sheep's clothing."

Creating Your Truth

Now that you know the attributes and qualities of your personal God and how your personal God relates to you, it's time to take the next step. You need to discover the Truth of who you are. It is important to come up with what I call a truth statement about you. This truth statement is what your personal God knows you truly to be. It is the true essence of your being.

Think of your own child or someone you love unconditionally. Others may define them through their seeming physical and emotional defects or flaws. Because of your unconditional love, you see them differently; you see the Truth of them. You do not define them through their seeming flaws or defects, but through your unconditional love for them. My own children have their destructive beliefs, and they and others may define and criticize them according to mistakes they have made or things they have done or how they look, but something deep within me knows them to be perfect just as they are. Love sees through the surface to the Truth of that which is loved.

I am an avid cat lover. When I was young, my mother became a breeder of Persian cats. I grew up with a constant flow of little animated fur balls. Not long after my first wife and I were married, we decided we needed some feline friends. One Columbus Day we visited a Persian cat breeder and came away with two little furry kittens, a male and a female, half-siblings. Since it was Columbus Day, we named them Ferdinand and Isabella, a.k.a., Furry and Lala. Being Persians, they had the pug faces and some other quirks that go along with the Persian breed. Furry had a crooked fang that pointed slightly outward instead of straight down. This condition prevented him from keeping his tongue in his mouth, and so its normal resting position was to stick slightly out of his mouth. The whole effect gave the poor kitty a witless look. I remember a visiting cousin exclaiming him to be the ugliest cat he had ever seen.

But I didn't see Furry that way. He was very loving and affectionate. He loved me through thick and thin. He loved me when I couldn't love myself and felt unloved by the whole world. I didn't see Furry as the ugliest cat I had ever seen. I loved that little cat with all my heart. My love and gratitude saw him as an angel of God. This was the Truth of Furry, my affectionate and loving pet cat. This is the truth statement for Furry the cat.

Just as I see the Truth of Furry and my children through my unconditional love for them, my personal God sees me in the same manner. My personal God loves me unconditionally and so knows the Truth of me through that unconditional love. My personal God sees me as "perfect," even though I may believe otherwise. This means that I know the answer to the question, Who am I? Which is, "I am a perfect, divine child of God." This is my truth statement about who I am.

You find your truth statement by getting in touch with the words that define the deeper Truth of your own children or some being you love unconditionally. Look at the qualities and attributes you have given your personal God about how your personal God relates to you. If you could choose or "make up" a wonderful truth statement about who you really are, what would it be? Find a short phrase that feels good to you and that captures the essence of how you want your own personal God to see you. It is important to come up with a positive statement that feels right for you and your personal God. Here are some short phrases to say. How do they feel when you say them? Come up with some of your own, but keep them generically positive like these examples.

- I am a perfect, divine child of God.
- I am a wonderful child of God. Period!
- I am a light of a wondrous God.
- I am God's pure love.
- I am God's pure light.
- I am the Joy of God.
- I am the light and love of my wonderful God.

I know that creating a truth statement about oneself in these positive terms can be near impossible for some people at first. If you are having a hard time with this, then feel free to make your truth statement more conditional. Here are the above truth statements rephrased into conditional form:

- I want to believe I am a perfect, divine child of God.
- It would be nice to believe I am a wonderful child of God.
- I am willing to come to believe I am a light of a wondrous God.
- I can't wait to believe I am God's pure love.
- Maybe I am God's pure light.
- What if I really am the joy of God?
- It would be great to know that I am the light and love of my wonderful God.

If you do what is asked of you in this chapter, you now have a list of qualities that define your personal God as well as a truth statement that defines you through the eyes of your personal God. If you are having a lot of resistance with this exercise, then try giving yourself permission by asking yourself, "If I could create a personal God, what qualities would I give it in relation to myself?" and "How would I want my personal God to think of me?" If you have trusted friends that understand what you are trying to do, then by all means enlist their help in this creative process. Have them repeat each of the sample truth statements as if they are your personal God. Notice how each feels when said directly to you. Pick the one that you feel most resonates with you.

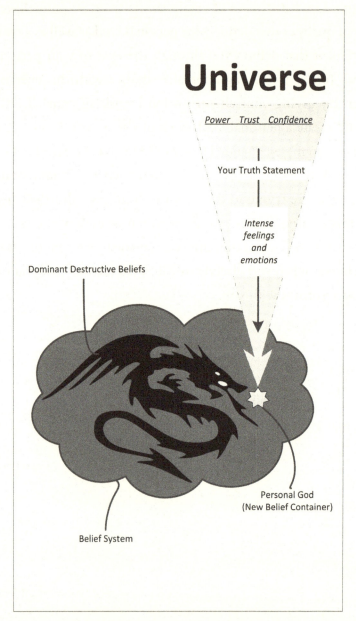

Figure 4.1. Creating your new belief container in your belief system

Knowing the Truth from the Lie

Bible wisdom: "And you shall know the truth, and the truth shall make you free" (John 8:32).

Bible wisdom: "Even so, every good tree bears good fruit; but a bad tree bears bad fruit. A good tree cannot bear bad fruit, nor can a bad tree bear good fruit" (Matthew 7:17–18).

This teaching gives us direction on how to know the truth from the lie. I will talk much more about this in the following chapters because knowing the truth from the lie will be our baseline gauge to know what is currently happening in our emotional dimension.

Understanding our feelings gives us information about which beliefs are actively engaged and whether they are destructive or constructive. I call our destructive beliefs the lie and our constructive beliefs the truth. According to the teaching from our Bible wisdom, the truth feels freeing and expansive. This means that the lie must feel binding and constrictive.

Try it out for yourself. Repeat one of the phrases from your destructive voices. For example, one of mine is, "I am the biggest piece of junk God ever created!" How does it feel when you say one of your destructive phrases to yourself? Try to feel it as when you are really believing what it is saying about you. Is what you feel light and expansive or binding and constrictive? Does it feel liberating or heavy and oppressive? When I say my destructive phrase to myself, it feels binding and constrictive, oppressive and depressing, very yucky! This is how I know that I am currently believing a lie generated by a destructive belief.

Now say your truth statement or something from the list of attributes and qualities that define your personal God. For example, my truth statement is, "I am a perfect, divine child of God, and God's will for me is to be prosperous in every aspect of my life!" Say your truth statement to yourself with as much belief and gusto as you can summon. How does it feel when you say your truth statement to yourself? Compare how you feel saying your truth statement to how you felt when you said one of your destructive phrases. When I say my truth statement to myself, it feels empowering and expansive. This tells me that I am in the Truth.

Take some time to practice testing the feelings associated with the statements from both your list of destructive voices and the phrases associated with your personal God. Remember that a good tree brings forth good fruit, and the Truth will set you free!

My first experience with a personal God seemed like a thunderbolt. The little seed that was planted in my emotional dimension had a dramatic effect on my beliefs. My life began changing quickly and dramatically. Within a couple of months, I was living in a recovery house in Atlanta, Georgia, working full time, and supporting myself financially. The impossible had suddenly become possible. Within a few years, I was a college graduate with a bachelor of science degree in applied physics, married, and a homeowner. I had come up with an invention and had actually written my own patent application. This led to a great professional job as a patent agent working for an intellectual law firm. All my dreams were literally coming true, but ...

I fell into the trap that I now know ensnares many. At first, I was so excited about the incredible things my personal God was doing for me that I put a lot of effort into building my faith and belief. As I got the things in life that I wanted, I started skimping on my relationship with my personal God and focusing more on my worldly worries. I did not know about the concepts I am presenting in this book. I was not aware of my destructive beliefs or how they were affecting and influencing my life. They had just gone dormant during my initial enthusiasm about finding my personal God. Now I was in a marriage relationship, had important financial responsibilities, and was soon to become a father. Fear, worry, and anxiety started creeping into my emotional consciousness. Holding onto the worldly things I had accumulated brought fear and worry back into the forefront of my life. Fear and worry presented an excellent opportunity for my destructive beliefs to make up for lost time.

Eventually the day came when everything blew up. My wife divorced me, my brother died, and I ended up losing most of my money trying to get rich quick in the stock market. I was now a penniless and jobless divorced father of two young children. All this slammed me hard, and I struggled for almost a year just to keep from killing myself. My destructive beliefs had taken full control, and I worshipped them with all my heart and soul. I was the biggest failure of a human being that ever existed or ever would exist. That was my mantra, and I hated myself to no end. The emotional pain was literally unbearable, and I felt it twenty-four hours a day, seven days a week. It was so bad that I had to be hospitalized several times during that year. I thought about returning to alcohol but knew it would just make things worse.

Something had to give, or I was a goner. The power of my destructive beliefs had broken something in my brain. I saw many doctors and psychiatrists, who tried all kinds of therapies and antidepressants but to no avail. I had resigned myself to an early grave when the miracle occurred. Fate had somehow put me at a hospital in a place I had not expected or planned. I was on my last legs figuring that nothing would be different this time around. The psychiatrist on staff called me in and actually reviewed my history with interest. I don't remember anyone actually bothering to do that before. He put me on a drug that he said was highly effective but rarely used anymore and explained how it worked and why it might be what would work for me. That medication and that doctor saved my life. Without going into details, I was not supposed to be in that hospital that day. The plan was for me to be somewhere else, but for some weird reason the plans got screwed up, and I ended up with that man in that place. I had been doing a lot of praying to my long lost personal God during those terrible times. Most of my prayers were desperate pleas for help. The wonderful relationship I had with my personal God so long ago had faded into obscurity but had not died.

Chapter 4 Important Concepts and Exercises

In this chapter, you actually create your new belief entity called your personal God and your truth statement. Your truth statement defines your relationship with your personal God—it is what your personal God knows to be the truth of you. Imagine you are holding your baby child in your arms. Your baby child is looking into your eyes with love and joy. You are looking into your child's eyes, and your heart is full of unconditional love. It is at these moments when you know and feel the Truth of your child. Now replace you with your personal God and your baby child with you. Your personal God is holding you in his/her arms and looking into your eyes and knowing and feeling the same truth of you as you were doing with your own child. This is the relationship you are building with your personal God.

In the previous chapter, you became aware of your destructive beliefs. Your destructive beliefs are really just a belief container holding another definition of you—a bad, self-hating definition of you. In effect, you have inadvertently created a personal Satan with a destructive definition of yourself, which you have come to believe is the truth of you. If you can create a personal Satan through which you define yourself, then why can't you do the same with a personal God? We will talk in more detail about this in the following chapters.

Important Exercises

Study the detailed exercises contained in this chapter and give yourself permission to create your personal God and your truth statement according to your deepest desires. Don't worry about believing in them right now; just let yourself create what you truly want.

CHAPTER 5

Expanding Your Personal Power

Before we go on, I want to reiterate what you are actually doing by creating and empowering your personal God. Foremost, this is not about changing the nonreligious to the religious or the religious to the nonreligious. It is about activating specific powers and forces that you already possess but that have been scattered into dissonance and obscurity by your destructive beliefs. Integrity, confidence, courage, conviction, passion, compassion, trust, reliance, responsibility, creativity, purpose, intelligence, and wisdom are the powerful qualities you find in your personal God. You are bringing in nothing from outside of you. It is totally an inside job!

Building Your Relationship with Your Personal God

Bible wisdom: "Therefore whoever hears these sayings of Mine, and does them, I will liken him to a wise man who built his house on the rock: and the rain descended, the floods came, and the winds blew and beat on that house; and it did not fall, for it was founded on the rock. But everyone who hears these sayings of Mine, and does not do them, will be like a foolish man who built his house on the sand: and the rain descended, the floods came, and the winds blew and beat on that house; and it fell. And great was its fall" (Matthew 7:24–27).

Once you have created the qualities and attributes for your personal God, then you need to continually nurture and build your relationship with your personal God. You do this in the same manner you built your faith in your destructive beliefs.

Your destructive beliefs are empowered by the intense feelings and conviction in which you believed in them. Every time they told you who you are or what you deserve in life, you believed with absolute faith. You gave them power, trust, and reliance every time you believed in them and backed up your belief with intense feeling and conviction.

You have to spend quality time with your new beliefs. You also have to integrate your personal God with the feelings that correspond with the beautiful attributes with which you have endowed your personal God. Use your powerful commitment to create the desired changes in your life and help you grow your faith and trust in your personal God. You need this resolve to do the hardest thing any human can do, intentionally change your beliefs. Your destructive beliefs were created subconsciously and therefore could grow in power without any conscious effort on your behalf. You were totally unaware of what you were doing. Creating new beliefs in conscious awareness is an endeavor that is much more difficult.

Your destructive beliefs are very jealous. They demand total power and are intolerant of any beliefs that may challenge their power. Just thinking about creating new beliefs in a personal God will severely threaten your destructive beliefs. Keep in mind that your destructive beliefs associate loss of power with death itself. These exercises will create a firestorm in your emotional dimension. Your destructive beliefs will struggle intensely against letting you create and build a belief that threatens their power. They will try to fool you by telling you that this personal God business is pure foolishness. They will fill your mind with doubt and fear to prevent you from creating and empowering your belief in your personal God. They will tell you how hopeless it is, and you will intensely feel that hopelessness. They will tell you it is impossible or stupid or that you don't have enough time or whatever. They know you much better than you know yourself and can summon all kinds of deeply buried thoughts and feelings that will sound completely logical and true to you, anything to prevent you from moving forward with this endeavor.

At this stage in the game, your belief in your personal God will be at a minimum; you are still very much at the mercy of your destructive beliefs. You are virtually defenseless against their power and might. If they feel that their power over your life is threatened, they can, and most likely will, attack with all the power and cunning at their disposal—power that you have given them over many years of believing in them. Creating and empowering your personal God may feel intensely threatening to you. This is because your old beliefs are threatened. If you let them squash the new seeds you are planting in your belief system, then you will remain stuck in the old beliefs without the ability to effect the changes you desire. This will have the effect of growing the power of your old destructive beliefs because they get to say, "See, I told you so; you can't do that; you fail every time!"

Make it a daily practice to engage and build your belief and trust in your personal God. A great way to start is by sitting quietly for a few minutes and thanking your personal God for being such a wonderful presence in your life. Feel this with as much intensity as you can muster. Make use of your list of qualities and attributes created in the previous chapter. For instance, if one of the attributes on your list is "God loves me absolutely, unconditionally, and eternally. Nothing I have done or will do can change God's absolute love for me," then you can simply say out loud or in your mind, "Thank you for loving me unconditionally and eternally." Feel your gratitude for being loved so deeply. Add intensity by celebrating these beautiful feelings! Do the same with the other attributes you have created.

I am very visual and will see a loving image with which I am communing. It could be an image of Jesus looking at me with an expression that conveys the love my personal God feels for me. Sometimes the image is a streaming light emanating from the darkness of the universe. I have even envisioned a giant hand holding me in a loving manner. Feel free to associate your personal God with an image that captures the essence of the words and feelings that you are using.

Start by doing this for a few seconds. Expect a lot of interference and mental jabbering. Remember, your destructive beliefs will not appreciate what you are doing and will try to sabotage your efforts by putting nasty thoughts and images in your mind. Remain indifferent by not fighting and struggling with whatever is going through your mind. I have come to laugh when this happens and say, "Wow, isn't that thought that just appeared very bizarre!" or "How interesting, that thought just called me a stupid idiot." When this happens, simply refocus by repeating your statement: "Thank you for loving me unconditionally and eternally!" or whatever statement you are using. If it gets too uncomfortable, then stop and go about your business. Success is simply the act of giving it a try. What happens or how long you do it is of no importance. Read books on meditation or techniques for quieting your mind. Stay the course and let yourself be profoundly surprised at how your life magically improves. Just keep doing this at least once a day. Eventually increase to morning and evening. The key is to make it a regular practice.

A great way to build trust in your personal God is to ask for guidance around making the right choices in your life. When you face a dilemma in your daily life, take time to sit quietly and ask your personal God for help and guidance concerning the right action to take. For instance, "God, help me to say what I need to say with confidence and courage," or "Guide me as I present my ideas to this person or group of people." Get used to asking for help and guidance on anything you need, small or large.

Make it a regular practice to sit quietly with your personal God and state your truth statement. For example, I will sit quietly and say to my personal God, "I am Your perfect, divine child," and smile as I feel my personal God affirming the truth of my statement. This is a wonderful way to build confidence and belief. It is vital to cement your truth statement into both your conscious and subconscious mind. Constantly repeating your truth statement with intense feeling and focus is the best way to accomplish this.

These exercises I am enumerating are great examples to help you get started. It is up to you to explore and experiment in order to discover what practices, meditations, and prayers resonate and feel best to you. The key is to continually build your belief in this power within yourself that we are calling your personal God. You are building a trust relationship with powerful forces deep within yourself.

As you do these exercises, things will start to work out better than you expected. It is vital that you give credit where credit is due. Acknowledge the help and guidance that was provided by your personal God. Acknowledging that your personal God came through for you builds your trust and belief in your personal God and encourages you to continue empowering your trust and belief. You may be tempted to assign the credit to coincidence or chance. This is just your destructive beliefs trying to prevent you from further empowering your personal God. Rely on fact and evidence. You started doing this, and then this happened—cause and effect.

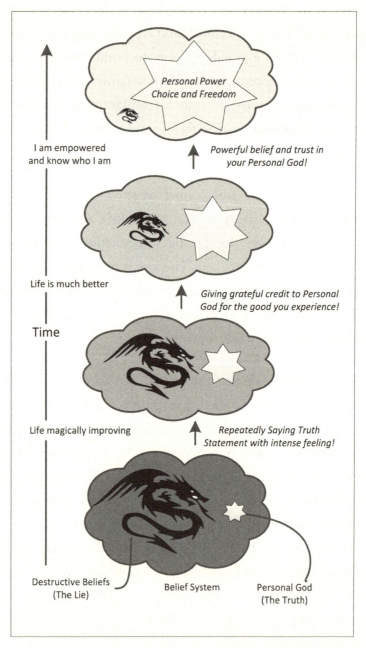

Figure 5.1. Building belief in your personal God

Building your belief and trust in your personal God opens up new realms of possibilities in your experience of life. As your new beliefs grow you start seeing more clearly and with more wisdom and awareness. You find yourself reacting differently to situations which brings new experiences into your life. The light of your new beliefs starts penetrating the dark shroud of your destructive beliefs. You are becoming more aware and seeing life's situations from a more enlightened perspective.

I experienced numerous moments of clarity and understanding as I built my faith and trust in my personal God. There were times when I was faced with situations that left me fearful and confused. I needed to make important decisions about my life but my old destructive beliefs were dominating my thinking and filling me with fear and doubt. During these times I would beg my personal God for help and guidance about what to do. I experienced many instances where I was filled with confidence, decisiveness, and energy after going to my personal God for help. It was very strange how people would just appear in my life at just the right time to provide me with the help I needed to overcome a difficult situation. There were also times when someone would mention something randomly in a conversation that turned out to be the answer to a problem I had not yet experienced. When the problem appeared, I would remember something someone had talked about in a previous conversation that was the exact answer I needed to take care of my difficulty in the best way possible. The answers came into my thoughts as I was asking my personal God for help and guidance during a time of fear and indecision about the actions I needed to take in my life.

As you keep growing in your belief in your personal God and your truth, your confidence in yourself and life grows accordingly. These changes will most likely be imperceptible. Eventually, you find yourself negotiating for a higher salary when before you would have taken the salary that the company offered up front. You begin to find that you will not accept being treated disrespectfully or disparagingly by certain people who got away with treating you that way in the past. Many little things about you that go unnoticed by you start changing for the better as you build you faith and trust in your personal God and your truth. One day you look back and notice that your life has changed immeasurably.

I can look back now and see the wonderful changes that have taken place in my life as I began to nurture my trust and belief in my personal God and my truth. When I would change jobs, I would take the salary that was offered because I was afraid that I would not get the job if I demanded a higher salary. I lacked confidence in my skills and abilities. As I continued to nurture and grow my faith and trust, eventually my confidence increased and I began to negotiate with the companies that wanted to hire me. My increased confidence in myself and my abilities also crept into the job interviews I attended. When I didn't get a job offer I would trust that my personal God had something better picked out for me around the next corner.

Instead of feeling dejected, I would be eager for the next opportunity that was soon to come. My confident attitude and trust in the future was a big change from the doubt and fear that used to rule my life before I started believing and trusting in my personal God and my truth statement.

Living in your destructive beliefs is living in constant fear. Life feels very threatening and the future is something to fear and avoid. When you feel threatened, you are unable to give freely of yourself. You can only take because fear is totally self-absorbing. As I grew in my trust and faith in my personal God and my truth, I wanted to become a more giving person. I wanted to start giving of myself without needing some return on my giving investment. I started to understand that becoming more of a "giver" than a "taker" would help me come to be more of the person I truly wanted to be. I came across the beautiful prayer of Saint Francis of Assisi in my reading and memorized it. I would say it every day to help me learn how to give more of myself to life. This helped me stay aware during my daily routine and find opportunities to have new experiences in life.

Trusting Your Personal God

Bible wisdom: "Blessed are those who mourn, for they shall be comforted" (Matthew 5:4).

Sometimes something big happens, such as divorce, loss of job, death of a loved one, and such things. We all have major losses in life that cause a great deal of emotional pain. During these times in my life, I have just had to keep asking my personal God to see me through and help me take the pain. Asking God to remove the pain or remove the situation would be asking God to turn me into something other than human. There are many things that happen in the physical world that I judge as bad or evil or wrong. The fact is that I just don't understand why these things happen. I see and experience an extremely thin slice of the infinite events that make up our physical universe. I have to concede that I just don't know why these things have to happen, and keep faith with my personal God.

In the summer of 2000, I got a call from my mother saying my brother was in the emergency room at the hospital. She was distressed because of the seriousness of my brother's situation and wanted me to come and help out. My brother was still in the emergency room when I arrived. They said he had a pretty nasty case of pneumonia. The first thing I noticed was my brother's fear, which confirmed how dangerous he felt the situation to be. He was scared that he was dying. In an effort to comfort him, I told him that pneumonia is a very common thing and not such a big deal. Experiencing his fear was painful to me, and I wanted to make it go away. I didn't ever remember seeing him act that way, which scared me quite a bit. Eventually, the doctor came with the results of the tests. The doctor said my brother had pneumocystis pneumonia, which is caused by a common fungus. The doctor wrote out some prescriptions and sent him home. I was relieved that no one seemed to think it was a big deal.

When I got home and told my wife about my brother's pneumonia, she immediately said that he had AIDS. I argued that he simply had a common variety of pneumonia, not AIDS. I was shocked that she would say such a thing! We were raised in a heterosexual middle class family, which meant it was impossible for my brother to have AIDS. Despite my denials, it wasn't long before my brother found out that he had AIDS.

AIDS is the stage of HIV infection in which your immune system has been compromised. You measure how bad things are by the viral load count and the immune system T-cell count. My brother's counts were such that certain death was imminent! A few months after the emergency room visit, he started losing physical motor function because the disease was eating away something in his brain. He just couldn't remember how to do simple things such as walk, stand up, sit down, etc. I kept forgetting that the connection between his will and his physical body was severed. I would tell him to get up, and he would just sit there. I would say it again before I understood that he couldn't figure out how to stand up, and I had to lead him to a standing position. Then I had to lead each foot forward because he forgot how to walk. Seeing my brother in such a pathetic condition was a major calamity for me. It was all so weirdly unreal. Eventually we had to move him into a hospice, where he died several months later—on Christmas

Day. Each Christmas Day since his death, my Christmas gift to him is to lovingly call him an SOB for having the audacity to die on Christmas Day.

This experience made me ask a lot of whys. Why is this happening to my brother? Why is this happening to my poor mother? My mother lost her father, and now her son! Why did my brother have to die that way? There were no answers to my questions. It just happened the way it happened.

I felt a lot of survivor guilt. I was the sexually promiscuous one in young adulthood. If one of us was to get AIDS, it should have been me. I also remember thinking that his death meant more financial inheritance for me. I burned with shame about having such an evil thought.

All I could do was be there for my brother and mother and experience my pain, sadness, anger, and guilt. This in itself was one of the blessings my personal God had bestowed upon me. When I was drinking and had no connection to my personal God, I doubt I would have been much help or comfort for my mother and brother. I asked my personal God for much help during this time. I remember being comforted by the thought that even though my brother died, God's will for me is still to have a happy and wonderful life—just like my will is for my own children. My personal God also helped me resolve the guilt I felt about having thoughts concerning the inheritance. I was experiencing financial woes at the time, and these thoughts were simply how those worries expressed themselves. It wasn't that I was bad or evil or that I wanted my brother to die so I could have a bigger financial inheritance. I truly loved my brother. He was only a year and a half older than me. We shared a bedroom and played together for most of our adolescence. Of my three older brothers, he was the one I was closest to.

I am using every argument at my disposal to encourage you to do what it takes to build some semblance of trust and belief in the personal God you have created. I am preparing you for the next chapter, wherein you will begin to challenge your destructive beliefs. If you try to take on one of these powerhouses without having procured a powerful ally, you will be knocked down hard and quick. This experience can easily break any resolve you have mustered and keep you down for the count, causing you to meekly crawl back to your destructive beliefs, never daring to challenge them again. Make sure you build your foundation on rock and not on sand.

David J. Saffold

Chapter 5 Important Concepts and Exercises

The important concept to understand from this chapter is that you must build and nurture the new beliefs you created in the previous chapter. You do this by connecting intense feelings with your thoughts and words because feelings provide the energy and power behind beliefs.

Important Exercises

Practice the exercises outlined in this chapter. Make them a regular practice and notice how things start improving, as if by magic.

Sit quietly for a few minutes and thank your personal God for being such a wonderful presence in your life. Feel this with as much intensity as you can muster.

Use your list of qualities and attributes created in the previous chapter to intensify your relationship with your personal God. For instance, if one of the attributes on your list is, "God loves me absolutely, unconditionally, and eternally. Nothing I have done or will do can change God's absolute love for me," then you can simply say out loud or in your mind, "Thank you for loving me unconditionally and eternally." Feel the intense gratitude that comes with saying this with belief and meaning.

A Beginner's Guide to Perfection

Start including your personal God in everything about your life. Expand your communication channel with your personal God by conversing with your personal God about anything and everything.

CHAPTER 6
Challenging Your Destructive Beliefs

Bible wisdom: "The thief does not come except to steal, and to kill, and to destroy. I have come that they may have life, and that they may have it more abundantly" (John 10:10).

In this chapter, we actually start the process of changing our beliefs. What we are really doing is redirecting our faith in our destructive beliefs to the new beliefs we have integrated into our personal God. We do this by our new awareness and the power of our words. We use our words by calling The Lie a lie and The Truth the truth. We make a powerful statement that we do not believe The Lie anymore and then state The Truth in which we now do believe. We use our awareness to know when our destructive beliefs are actively telling us a lie about ourselves. For instance, when I hear my destructive beliefs tell me I am a nothing or a failure or one of the other statements on my destructive voices list, I immediately say, "That's a lie, I don't believe you anymore." Then I say my truth statement, *"I am a perfect divine child of God!"*. I say my truth statement with intense feeling and conviction. The more conviction I use, the more powerful the effect.

Redirecting the Power of Your Belief

Each time you tell your destructive beliefs that they are a lie and that you don't believe what they are saying to you, their power over your life is diminished. Each time you immediately say your truth statement in response to your destructive beliefs, your belief in your truth statement is enhanced. This effectively redirects the power of your belief from your destructive beliefs to your personal God and the new beliefs you have created. As your power flows from your destructive beliefs toward your personal God, your experience of life changes accordingly. It is important to keep your truth statement connected to the destructive belief that just attacked you by immediately and directly responding with your Truth.

Using the Energy of Anger

Anger is a great source of energy that, when directed appropriately, can help you stand up to and challenge the power of your destructive beliefs with significantly enhanced force and confidence. What if, one day, some nasty little being knocked on your door claiming to be a long-lost relative? Before you knew it, this nasty, vulgar relative is living in your house and following you around everywhere you go. Worse still, it starts screwing up everything you try to accomplish in your life by constantly telling you what a miserable piece of dung of a human being you are. You want to date a nice person, and your nasty companion fills your head with how there is no way a nice someone like that would want the likes of you. You dream of starting your own business, and here comes your nasty little relative telling you, "No way. Don't even think about it; you are way too stupid to do something like that." This nasty little relative just can't say enough about how ugly, or stupid, or bad, or undeserving, or guilty you are. It's all your nasty little relative talks about.

This nasty, vulgar, hateful, little thing took up residence in your house uninvited and is making your life miserable, and you sit there and take this kind of treatment. What is it going to take for you to decide to kick the living daylights out of this horrible little creep? You didn't invite this nasty little creep into your life, and here it is sleeping in your very bed, eating your food, and making your misery and failure its sole mission in life.

Get mad! Get very mad! Get so mad you decide with every enraged cell in your body that this will not stand! Get so mad that you snag that little wretch up by the collar and tell it that it is out of your life right now, and that if you ever even think you see it, you will hunt it down and twist its scrawny little head off its neck.

Whew, yes, anger can definitely be a great energy source when challenging your destructive beliefs. Like everything relating to your emotional dimension, intensity of emotion or feeling is the key ingredient. Anger can help you take your power back. When I got in touch with the voices of my destructive beliefs, I eventually noticed the confidence they embodied. They declared who I was and what would happen with confidence and certainty. The power flowed one way, from them to me. I had no power, like a small child facing a stern and abusive parent. When I finally got mad, the balance of power shifted. Now I was the one speaking with confidence and conviction to my cowering destructive beliefs.

A Beginner's Guide to Perfection

The Power of Your Truth Statement

I will never forget that day when I got mad. I was doing a lot of inner spiritual work after finally rising up from the emotional collapse I experienced after my divorce. I had come up with my truth statement of being a perfect, divine child of God and was working on my belief that this was the truth of me. I had also recently become aware of my destructive voices and how they were affecting my life. I was still a little feeble admitting I was a perfect, divine child of God, so one day I decided to say it to myself while facing my bathroom mirror. I was trying out some different techniques to build belief in my truth statement.

So I mumble "I am a perfect, divine child of God" to myself in the mirror, and suddenly everything explodes! It was like a huge dragon rises up and says, "How dare *you* say such *blasphemy!*" This scares the living daylights out of me. I had enraged something big time, and it will have none of it. So here I am, little me, facing this huge fire-breathing dragon, which is ready to shred me to pieces if I even think defiance, much less actually be defiant.

Then I get mad, real mad! I tell it that I will not back down even if one of us has to die right here, right now. My anger is so intense that it knows I mean every word. And I do mean it, because I am so mad that I will die if that's what it takes because I am sick of being a man with no confidence and no power. I draw my imaginary sword and yell, "Let's go at it, you son of a b★★★. It's a great day to die!"

Then something weird happened. All of a sudden, this monstrous powerhouse of a beast that had wielded so much power over me for so long just up and collapsed into a little cloud of smoke. I stood there, sword in hand, staring at what turned out to be nothing. I finally saw reality! There was nothing that had power over me except for what I had given that power. My monster, or destructive beliefs, were simply that—beliefs. They had no power except for the power that I gave them by believing in them. When I directly faced the power of my destructive beliefs and claimed my truth without backing down, my destructive beliefs had no option but to reveal their true selves. I had taken back my power, and my destructive beliefs deflated accordingly. Without the power that I give them, they are simply thoughts—nothing.

This experience whipped my anger into a fury. The energy released enabled me to stay hyperaware for several weeks. I started hunting my destructive beliefs, daring them to come out and face me. When one made the mistake of daring to challenge me, I would tear it to pieces and throw its remains back down into perdition. Each encounter proved to me that they were powerless in reality, and grew my confidence and trust in my personal God and in myself. Eventually I calmed down as my destructive beliefs became too afraid to face me head-on anymore. My bizarre and ferocious behavior confounded them such that they felt it necessary to retreat back into the woodwork. They were at a loss due to their rapid fall from grace and the sudden power shift that had redefined our relationship.

This experience showed me the power of my truth statement! I started saying my truth statement to myself with more confidence and belief, more power and feeling. Eventually I had no shame in claiming who I was to myself. As my confidence and belief grew, I was able to tell other individuals, with confidence and power who I was when it seemed appropriate. Next thing I know, I am able to tell audiences of people who I am with confidence and conviction. As my beliefs changed, I became more of a person of confidence and integrity. This had a big effect on my life. I earned more money and gained better positions in my work life. My dating life was easier as I became less fearful and more confident. My interactions and relationships with others changed for the better as I became much better at saying what I wanted and what was acceptable and not acceptable. Every aspect of my life began to change toward that which I really wanted. Best of all, I started feeling a sense of purpose in my life. I didn't know where any of this was leading me, but I know I liked the new road I was now traveling much better than the one I was on before.

Don't get me wrong; these changes were not instantaneous but more of an ever-widening trend. I still had a lot of work to do challenging my destructive beliefs and building my beliefs in my personal God. What happened that day with that dragon was a beginning, not an end. It was my decision to turn my faith and allegiance toward my personal God and away from my destructive beliefs.

When I am working with others, I usually ask them who they are. Usually, they have never been asked this before and have certainly never thought about it. When answering this question, most define what they do: "I am a mother, father, manager, worker," this or that job title, etc. They might also say, "I am Joe or Jane" some-name. I smile when I see their eyes go blank as their minds try to understand the question. Who you are is *the most important thing you should know*! Who you are touches everything about your life and your experience of life.

Bible wisdom: "But he who does the truth comes to the light, that his deeds may be clearly seen, that they have been done in God" (John 3:21).

When you look closely at your destructive beliefs and the words they use against you, then you will notice that what they are actually doing is defining you. For instance, when you want to try to realize some burning ambition, your destructive belief might pop up and say, "Don't bother; you will fail as usual!" or something similar, and it zaps you with feelings of futility and hopelessness. What this destructive belief is really saying to you is, "You *are* a failure!" It is saying that who you are is a failure, which means that you have always failed and always will fail because you have always been and will always be a failure. There is a big difference between "You will fail at this particular endeavor" and "You are a failure." "You will fail at this particular endeavor" is a conditional statement about the expected outcome of this particular endeavor. "You are a failure" is a defining statement about *you*! The feelings of futility and hopelessness indicate that you believe the underlying definition of yourself conveyed by your destructive beliefs. These feelings siphon off the energy of your initial feelings of confidence, conviction, and drive. The end result is the inability to follow through on your ambition.

This is why your truth statement is a vital ingredient when challenging your destructive beliefs. You need to build your belief in the truth of who you are before you can effectively challenge the old tried and true definitions that your destructive beliefs have used against you so effectively. If anger doesn't work for you, then use as much conviction as you can muster. When you feel and/or hear the destructive voices, sternly tell them you don't believe them anymore because they are lies, and you know who you are. Then say your truth statement with belief and conviction. Every time you do this, you change the balance of power between you and your destructive beliefs and diminish the fear they use to control you. Over time, you believe more and more that you *are* your truth statement, and the power that your destructive beliefs hold over you weakens accordingly. Eventually they become more of a nuisance than a real threat.

Do the same thing when your destructive beliefs speak to something specific. For instance, in my example above about realizing an ambition, when your destructive belief tells you that you will fail, then sternly say, "That is a lie, and I don't believe a word of it!" Then say the "Truth" that you get from your relationship with your personal God. For instance, you can say, "God's will for me is to realize my dreams and ambitions! Thank you, God!" Believe the "Truth" and feel it as intensely as you can. Feel the gratitude of knowing that your powerful and wonderful personal God wants wonderful things for your life, that your personal God is overjoyed about you realizing your dreams and ambitions, just as you would want your own beloved child to realize his or her dreams and ambitions in life.

Building awareness

At first, it is hard to become aware of the destructive beliefs and the destructive words they use to keep you in their power. The feelings and words they use have become so familiar that you simply see them as you. Ask your personal God for help with exposing them to your conscious awareness. Ask your personal God to help you become aware of the feelings and words they use to keep you in their power. Keep praying for help with this, and you will come to know when they are active. You will come to hear their words so you can directly challenge them.

Another way to become aware is to sit quietly and practice saying your truth statement. Odds are that you activated some of your destructive beliefs when practicing in the last chapter. When saying your truth statement, watch and listen with vigilance. You may feel tense or threatened. Don't try and make it stop, but investigate the feelings and thoughts. Where in your body do you feel it most? What exactly are the feelings you are feeling? What is happening in your conscious mind? What do you see and what do you hear? Take the feelings in your body and pretend to ball them up in your hands and push them a few feet out in front of you. What do they look like? You can ask them what they are and try to get them to speak to you and reveal their identities. These practices will build your awareness and help you become familiar with the destructive beliefs that are dominating you. This awareness gives you the ability to begin taking back your power.

Bible wisdom: "Yea, though I walk through the valley of the shadow of death, I will fear no evil; For You are with me; Your rod and Your staff, they comfort me" (Psalms 23:4).

A very powerful method for confronting your destructive beliefs is to face yourself in a mirror and say your truth statement. It is a good idea to have a solid connection with your personal God when performing this exercise. You need to be highly prepared since you could end up facing a full onslaught by your destructive beliefs. Don't push it unless you feel you are ready and can handle the powerful feelings that your destructive beliefs can generate. If you try this and it is too much, then simply walk away and shake it off. Thank your personal God for giving you the courage to give it a try. You can try it again after you have built more belief and trust in your personal God.

When I was challenging my destructive beliefs, I discovered that they used fear to maintain their power over my life. Fear is a very powerful emotion because it can warp your perception of reality and cause you to react destructively to events that are not truly threatening. One of my destructive beliefs was that I was a financial failure. I was terrified of going broke and my destructive beliefs used my fear to great advantage. As I began to have success challenging my destructive beliefs, I became able to tolerate the fear when it struck without reacting destructively. This ability enabled me to choose a different reaction to the events that were triggering my fear. I could choose a more constructive course of action or decide to take no action at all.

My expanded awareness enabled me to look more closely at the fear that was creating so much destruction in my life. When I was under the domination of my destructive beliefs and they determined that an event meant I was going broke, I believed it without question. When I became more aware and able to look more closely at this dynamic I saw how absurd it really was. There was no context or evidence that I was really going broke or in real danger of failing financially. My destructive beliefs never seemed to be based on real and verifiable evidence. The terror that I felt said I was going to lose all and die, but was that really true? I began questioning the veracity of what my feelings of fear were saying to me. If I did go broke, what would happen? Well, I guess I would have to go and live with my mother until I could get back on my feet. So, going broke was not the real monster that my destructive beliefs made it out to be. By the way, I may have come close to going broke at certain times in my life but I always made it through those rough economic times one way or the other. I came to see that my destructive beliefs were always based on pure fiction and contained no basis in reality. They were great at saying this or that terrible thing was going to happen, but had no evidence to back up and prove their claims about my future.

The methods I have suggested in this chapter are very powerful and will help you reclaim your power. However, you must practice them, build on them, and incorporate them into your daily routine. It is hard, at first, to hold the intense concentration and focus required to expand your awareness. As you progress, grow, expand, and build, it becomes easier and easier. A day will come when the power, confidence, courage, and Truth that is your personal God is also you.

Figure 6.1. Challenging your destructive beliefs

Chapter 6   Important Concepts and Exercises

The important concept to understand from this chapter is that each time you challenge your destructive beliefs with your truth statement, you are redirecting power from your destructive beliefs to your personal God and new beliefs. It is important to keep your truth statement connected to the destructive belief that just attacked you by immediately and directly responding with your Truth.

Tell your destructive beliefs that they are a lie and that you don't believe a word of what they are telling you. Say this with stern power and conviction. Then state the Truth of you, your truth statement, with intense feeling. The more conviction and feeling you use, the more powerful the effect. Afterward, thank your personal God for giving you the power to keep your truth.

Let yourself use your anger when confronting your destructive beliefs. Anger is a powerful source of energy and intense feeling—the stuff that builds belief.

Important Exercises

Do the exercises suggested in this chapter. Experiment with other ways to help you become aware of your destructive beliefs and effectively challenge them. Notice how the power balance starts shifting the more you become aware and the more you challenge your destructive beliefs.

Vigilance and awareness are the keys when challenging your destructive beliefs. At first you must exert a lot of energy to stay vigilant, but over time it will become easy and natural.

CHAPTER 7
Rebirth

Bible wisdom: "That which is born of the flesh is flesh; and that which is born of the Spirit is spirit. Marvel not that I said unto thee, Ye must be born again" (John 3:6-7).

When you create new beliefs, old beliefs must die away to make room for the new beliefs. You have been reborn into the new beliefs. You are literally a different person in terms of the new beliefs, and your life must change to accommodate the difference. Your new beliefs change how you experience the world. You are like a newborn baby in a new world. Things will seem strange until you explore and understand the new world that your new beliefs have exposed.

How Rebirth Works

Several years ago, I landed a job at a midsized company. I created an automated computer system that impressed the higher-level brass. This made my boss feel somewhat threatened. She started harping on my personal phone calls, saying I made too many, or they were too long. She also pointed out that I was talking to other employees too much. I apologized and told her I would limit my phone calls. However, no matter what I did, she kept getting on to me about this or that, and I kept trying to make her happy by telling her I would do better.

Nothing I could do to conciliate my boss's criticism solved her problem because the problem was her feelings of threat and not my behavior. This dynamic constantly repeated itself as I tried to appease her wrath with apologies and promises, but to no avail. My fear and lack of confidence in myself had inadvertently helped set up a parent-child relationship with my boss. My boss was the angry mother, and I was the bad little child. I saw this one day sitting in my cube feeling anxious. I started wondering why I felt so anxious and began asking my personal God what was going on. It soon occurred to me that I had felt this particular anxious feeling before. It was the same feeling I had as a child when I had done something "bad" and knew Mama was going to find out and be really angry with me.

When I made that connection, I saw exactly what was happening. I also saw how I was playing the part of a powerless child. As I sat there communing with my personal God about this, I saw how I had set up this same dynamic in the past. I also saw the destructive way it had been impacting my life. It was like I was raised to the top of a mountain peak, and could clearly see my life history and all the destruction this dynamic created in my life. Being the powerless child in a grown-up world had destructively affected my jobs, my income, my marriage, and all my endeavors to realize my ambitions and create the life I really desired.

Right then, I made a powerful decision that I did not want to be that man-child anymore. I prayed to my personal God to help me be the man that I wanted to be and that I knew my personal God wanted me to be. Not five minutes later, my boss came over to my cube, hands on hips with an angry look on her face, and said that we need to have a talk. Now that I was seeing reality, it was hilarious! She looked just like an angry parent addressing a wayward child. She ordered me to follow her to the conference room nearby—another moment of hilarity as I walked behind her to the conference room like a bad child on the way to the paddle room.

As I walked with her to the conference room, I remembered my decision and was confronted with a choice. Am I going to be the old man or the new man? I chose the new man with all my heart! This is how my new beliefs began affecting my life. We begin to have choices. The old man didn't have a choice because he had little confidence in himself. If a person with authority in his life said he was bad or wrong, then he was bad or wrong, in trouble like a child. Because I had changed my beliefs, I had the option of being the new man, an empowered man of confidence. It seemed as if life was testing my new beliefs to see if I really believed them. Life wasn't testing me; my new beliefs and awareness had given me another way to be where none had been before.

When we got to the conference room, she said that another manager had told her that I had been on personal calls the whole time she was on vacation. She had been out on vacation the previous week. Here is where things get interesting because her statement meant that I was on the phone for five days, eight hours a day. This ridiculous statement meant that she was speaking from her emotional state, from her feelings of threat and fear. The old me would have not seen this reality and just apologized and groveled. The new me saw through her statement in an instant.

Right after she said this, I retorted in a stern manner with, "That is a lie! You go get that person, and we will straighten this out right now!" This powerful and confident response caught her off guard and stunned her. She was expecting a child but got an adult of power and confidence. All she could do was mumble that maybe the other manager didn't say what she said he said. The power balance had shifted dramatically, and she didn't know how to handle this unexpected situation. I ended our little meeting with words of compassion, telling her that there is nothing wrong with making personal calls sometimes and talking and cutting up with other employees. I admonished her, saying that she should lighten up and not be so anxious about her work situation.

After our encounter in the conference room, I went back to my cube and thought about what had just happened. I felt guilty because I believed I had hurt her feelings. Acting on my feeling of guilt, I went over to her cube to apologize, but she was not there. It occurred to me that my old self was trying to pull me back and thanked God that she was not at her cube. I had done nothing wrong, and so no apology was needed. Again, I had to choose the new over the old. I decided to let her be responsible for whatever feelings she was experiencing resulting from the actions she had committed.

This is how rebirth happens. There is a period of exploration of the new while the old is still clinging on for dear life. The new feels strange and unknown while the old feels safe and known, making it easy to slide back into old behavior. The big difference is that you are aware. You have glimpsed the new and know when you have fallen back into the old. You have not failed by experiencing this sporadic movement between the old and new. It is just how these emotional rebirths tend to happen. Each time you choose the new over the old, your new world becomes more familiar, and you solidify your beliefs in the new you. One day, you look back at the old you, and what you see is a blurred dream of someone else living in another world. You know that you are not that person anymore and haven't been for a long time.

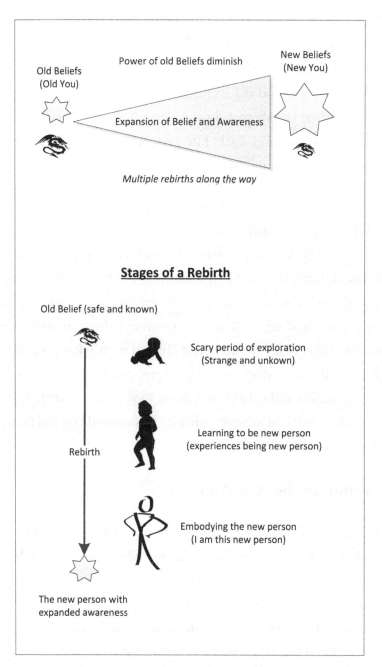

Figure 7.1. Process of rebirth

In an instant, my relationship with my boss changed dramatically. I became empowered and would no longer accept being a victim of other people's destructive beliefs, or my own. Now I decided when and if I had done something wrong and quit letting others decide that for me. Once I chose to be the new man, I could never go back. Life gave me a choice, and I chose. I had been reborn into the new.

The new confident and empowered person felt strange for a while. I had to learn to talk and act like this new person. I began feeling relaxed in job interviews because I was confident in my abilities. If I was asked something I didn't know, I would say I didn't know. The old me would try to make something up for fear of not doing well in the interview. I also started passing up job offers that I felt were not aligned with what I wanted. Best of all, I started asking for more pay and benefits because I was confident and valued my talents, experience, and abilities. The old me would just take what he was offered and feel lucky that he got the job.

Becoming the New You

As you become the new person, you see things you could not see before. For instance, the old me would believe people when they blamed me for their painful feelings. I would feel guilty and try to make them feel better. I didn't know that these people were simply trying to manipulate me to do something they wanted me to do. Because I was rooted in guilt and fear, I attracted these people and experiences. As I transitioned into the new, I saw that if I was truly responsible for their feelings, I would get credit for their good feelings as well as blame for their painful feelings. I don't remember ever getting credit for their good feelings! I also saw how certain people were using guilt as a way to control me. I came to see the reality of situations that I could not see before.

The old me was blind to the reality of most situations because I was rooted in the lie of my destructive beliefs. The new me clearly saw reality because I was rooted in the truth of my personal God and my new beliefs. The old problem disappeared when I was reborn into the new because people who needed a victim intuitively sensed that I was not that person.

My career was not the only part of my life that improved. A year or so after my divorce, I decided to start looking for my lifelong partner. I knew that I wanted a serious relationship that would hopefully lead to marriage. I didn't have a lot of experience dating and really didn't go to bars and those sorts of places, so I signed up on some of the internet dating services. Being new to internet dating, I experienced a lot of comedic tragedy before I got the hang of how it works. Internet dating is literally a series of blind dates, which produced a field day for my destructive beliefs. All my destructive beliefs around my attractiveness to women showed up: fear of rejection, my personal appearance, my financial status.

However, there was one big difference! I had belief and trust in my personal God. I would challenge my destructive beliefs as soon as they came into my awareness. I stayed grounded in my truth statement and my belief and trust in my personal God. I held onto the Truth of what my personal God wanted for my life in terms of a loving partner. On the way to meeting someone for the first time, I would repeat these "Truths" to myself and incorporate their power into my being. This enabled me to feel confident and comfortable being my true self with people. Confidence and authenticity made me more attractive to the type of person I wanted to end up dating and eventually marrying. This created an enjoyable experience when dating because I didn't fear being rejected. In fact, I came to see that the only person that can reject me is me.

Don't get me wrong; there were times when I fell back into fear, especially when I was very attracted to someone. But I would come out of these experiences having learned something important. I saw that no matter what happened, my personal God would do for me what I could not. I came to understand that my personal God wanted what's best for me even when I thought I knew what was best. When I tried to cling onto someone I desperately thought was "the one," it would fall apart for some reason or another. This was my personal God helping keep me out of relationships that were not suited for either party. When things didn't work out, I knew that it was because my personal God had something better waiting around the next corner.

I was single for seven years. During that time, I had a lot of rebirths. I kept growing in my new beliefs, and in my faith and trust in my personal God. All the experiences I was having were transforming me into the person that could have the life I truly desired. Like a wonderful preacher told me, "You have to be what you want." When I became enough of the new person I finally met the woman my personal God had waiting around the next corner.

Kim was attractive and successful in her career. The old me would have felt too inadequate and passed over her internet profile, but I had changed considerably. We corresponded for a little while and then met in person. We really liked each other and started dating with gusto. It was wonderful, but I started getting very scared. My old destructive beliefs found a chink in my armor. I wanted a serious relationship with her so much that I lost my dependence on my personal God. This is common when you are changing from the old to the new, and is a tried and true trick used by our destructive beliefs to regain power.

Intimate romantic relationships are the most emotionally disturbing relationships you can have. The reason is that these relationships require you to share all three of your dimensions with another person—physical, emotional, and spiritual. We expose all of our selves to another person, and this brings out our deepest and most powerful destructive beliefs. Rejection at this level is terrifying because you feel it means that someone who has experienced all of you didn't like what they found.

At least, this belief is what gives tremendous power to our destructive beliefs. This is why there is so much trauma and abuse in intimate romantic relationships and why your emotions can soar to the heavens one moment and be in the horrible abyss the next.

With Kim, my destructive beliefs made a big resurgence. She made a lot more money than I did. I didn't do bad, but that didn't matter. My destructive beliefs tricked me into believing that this was proof that I was a failure in Kim's eyes. It wouldn't be long before Kim would reject me. This destructive belief affected me so much that I almost caused her to break up with me. It was at this pivotal moment that I came back to reliance on my personal God. After this, I was calmer and was able to tell Kim about the fears I was experiencing. This honesty brought us closer together, contrary to what my destructive beliefs told me.

We were married a year later and are still happily married. We have had ups and downs like most, but we are both rooted enough in our personal God to come through the downs with flying colors. The more we both grow in the truth of ourselves and each other, the more we grow in our love. The relationship we have built, and are still building, is the relationship I truly desire and is an answer to my most fervent prayers. This proved to me that my personal God truly does love me and wants what's best for me. It also showed me that even when my destructive beliefs have knocked me down, my personal God always picks me up, faces me in the right direction, wipes my tears, comforts my fears, eases my pain, and holds me close.

Letting Go of the Old You

The new person you become must eventually let go of the old. This means that old friends that are not aligned with your new beliefs will start dropping away. Usually there is a period of struggling as you hang onto certain people that you may be afraid to let fall out of your life. Eventually something will happen, or the pain will become too much, and you let go. Usually, this happens gradually. As time goes on, your interactions with certain people diminish and eventually just stop altogether. You are making room for new people to come into your life that are more aligned with your new beliefs. You are a new person with a different character and new interests. You attract people that match the brighter energy that you are displaying. The behavior of others that was once acceptable becomes unacceptable. Work environments, colleagues, and bosses may become painful, which is a sign that these people and environments are not aligned with you anymore.

Ask and You Will Receive

Bible wisdom: "Jesus answered and said unto them, 'Assuredly I say to you, if you have faith, and do not doubt, you will not only do what was done to the fig tree, but also if you say to this mountain, be removed and be cast into the sea; it will be done. And whatever things you ask in prayer, believing, you will receive'" (Matthew 21:21–22).

A beautiful realization is to see that your personal God will give you what you ask, not just the big stuff but the little things too. All you have to do is ask, and the answer will come in one form or another. When you are reborn in your new beliefs and your personal God, your awareness of life expands to expose many more possibilities for your life. What once seemed impossible has come into the realm of the possible. Your expanded awareness and belief in your personal God enables you to recognize and accept the answer to that which you have asked. Fear and desperation is not what this is about. This is not a get rich quick scheme. Those types of things are not aligned with a true faith in your personal God and are rooted in destructive beliefs. However, amazing things do happen when you ask your personal God for good things in your life.

When my son, Isaac, was around ten years old, he really wanted the next generation DS, a handheld video game player. His younger sister had just gotten one for her birthday, which made him feel left behind with his old model. I explained to him that if he just believed, it would happen. I was not going to shell out the $120 needed to buy him one. He could ask his personal God to give him one or wait the many months till his next birthday. He started saying he was going to get one real soon. He was on fire with his belief and drive. He tried selling some of my old luggage to people living in our neighborhood. He got no takers but didn't get discouraged.

One night I mentioned my son's burning desire for a new DS to a friend while we were conversing on the phone. She said there was a store in town that would give cash for his old model. I casually mentioned this to my son, and he demanded that we go as soon as possible. I felt bad because I knew they would not give him nearly enough money for the old model that is required to get the new model. He begged, so I gave in and told him we would go first thing in the morning. Next day we showed up at the store, and the clerk said he would give around thirty dollars for his old DS. Then my daughter chimed in and said that he could have her old model. That was another thirty bucks or so. The store clerk asked if we had any games that went with these old models. We got the bag out of the car and plopped down a mass of the little game wafers. I figured he would give a few cents for each one, but he needed some time to do his figuring, so we walked around the store for a while. He called us over after a few minutes and said he would give us $120 for the whole lot, the two old model players and all the games. I almost fell down! That was the exact price of the new model! My son believed without doubt and became the proud owner of a new model DS player. Wow!

I remember praying for help to get in better physical shape. I was regularly exercising but wanted to do something to deflate the spare tire I was carrying around my midsection. I decided to ask my personal God for help. Sure enough, I got an email from the company fitness center a few days later. The fitness center was advertising an upcoming "Biggest Loser" contest, which would last for around three months and include daily classes, journaling, and homework. The email further described the class as extremely physically arduous with total intolerance for the uncommitted. You had to do what was demanded for the entire time allotted.

Well, that was a little too much for me, but wait, hadn't I just asked my personal God for help? Aha, the answer! I signed up, and sure enough, was in much better shape three months later. In fact, this experience propelled me to include running as part of my regular exercise routine. I had never thought of myself as a runner before. Adding running to my weekly exercise routine has kept me in better physical shape than ever before.

After my divorce, I found myself depressed and jobless. I did a lot of praying for help. My personal God took care of the depression as I explained earlier, but I still needed an income. I had been an engineer working for manufacturing companies prior to my divorce but hated those jobs. I just couldn't find any motivation to go back to doing that for a living. But what other skills did I have? What other career could I move into? I fervently asked my personal God for help around all this. I was not feeling very confident in myself so I would have to rely on my personal God root and branch.

At the time, I was living in a rental house with a roommate. Tom was a divorcee who I had met at an AA meeting. We became fast friends and decided to split the cost of renting. When I would wail about my awful situation, he loved to tell me to "just do the next right thing." This frustrated me for a while because I didn't feel like I knew what was "the next right thing." However, I soon realized it was part of the answer to my prayers. When I would go way out into the future and try to figure everything out, I would sink into fear, confusion, and depression. "The next right thing" helped me stay in the moment and focused on the next little step. When I stayed focused on that next little step, I actually accomplished something and felt good about my accomplishment. The next right thing became asking people about job opening at nearby companies. Eventually I got word that a company nearby was looking for factory line workers and paid a pretty decent hourly wage. I had much shame about doing a job I felt was beneath my talents and education level, but something within felt that applying was "the next right thing" in my current psychological situation.

The job was in a small town nearby, so off I went. I could not remember how to get to the state highway that led to this particular small town, so I pulled over into the nearest parking lot to check my map. This was before GPS-enabled cell phones and Google Maps, so I needed to consult my paper map. While stopped in the parking lot, I looked up and read the sign on the building. I was in the parking lot of a satellite office of the United States Department of Agriculture Farm Service Administration (USDA FSA). I didn't really know what that meant, but something powerful within me told me to go inside and ask for a job. I felt a little ridiculous but obeyed. The rest is literally on the scale of the miraculous. Things happened, people I didn't know intervened, and a little while later, I was working for the USDA FSA, helping build their geographical information system (GIS)—this is like a Google Maps for farmland but was before Google Maps came onto the internet scene. This led to a new career in computer programming and database development. It wasn't long before I was making more money in this career than I did in my previous career as an engineer in manufacturing. Best of all, I enjoyed the endless possibilities for creativity that it entailed.

When I look back at these events in my life, I have to give all the credit to my personal God. Once again, I proved to myself that my personal God is very real and powerful. Back then I was a wreck of a man with very little hope for a decent future. The only option I could summon was to throw myself totally on the dependence of my personal God. I had nothing else! I was a thirty-five-year-old man with a college degree and the career experience of a patent agent and an engineer—careers I never enjoyed and to which I could not return. The only thing I could think of was to apply for any job that was being offered. My only hope was that whatever job I found would be a little better than working at a fast-food restaurant. Boy, did I feel like a huge failure in life! The outcome turned out to be something I could never fathom from the view of life I had at the time. I had never heard of GIS or the USDA FSA and had no clue about computer programming or database systems. All I had to do was trust in my personal God and do the next right thing as best I could. No plan I could invent about the future came close to that which my personal God created for me, one step at a time.

These examples from my experience show what trust and belief in your personal God can do for your experience of life. The answer will be given. All you have to do is have the awareness to see the answer and say yes. Prayer has a way of focusing your awareness and opening you up to the myriad of possibilities that are always occurring around you.

The Ways of Rebirth

There were times in my life when I needed to make a painful decision. My destructive beliefs were filling me with fear and confusion, which was keeping me stuck and indecisive. It is then that I turned to my personal God, praying for help about what to do. I have experienced times when a powerful shift occurred deep within resulting in focused decisive action. In an instant, I knew exactly what to do, who to contact to help me do it, and the motivation and energy to act quickly and decisively. The fear and doubt vanished completely, and my energy soared to such heights that I actually became eager to act. One second I was despondent, full of fear and doubt, and the next second I was filled with confidence and chomping at the bit to take the action that had been revealed.

Rebirth is a process that happens in many different ways. There are times when you may experience dramatic shifts into the new. There are lulls where you feel that not much is changing. There are periods where you feel like you are floating in limbo with no discernible path to follow. There are also times of slow and steady enlightenment, the kind of growth that is hidden from you and only revealed when a friend or loved one mentions that you are somehow different than before. Building trust and faith in your personal God means you are always building potential that will bear good fruit.

Bible wisdom: "The lamp of the body is the eye. If therefore your eye is good, your whole body will be full of light. But if your eye is bad, your whole body will be full of darkness. If therefore the light that is in you is darkness, how great is that darkness!" (Matthew 6:22–23).

Consider the power of the sun. It is so bright that you cannot look at it directly. Its power is far too intense for you to bear without a filter. This is how it is with your personal God. Your personal God wields the immense power of the universe. You would blow up if you took in all that power at once. You, a mere human of little belief, are too small to contain the immense power flowing through your personal God. Your lack of belief and awareness is your filter. Expanding your belief and awareness enables you to handle more of that light, energy, and power. The light, energy, and power that flow from your personal God into you is reflected out into your life. You literally become brighter to other people as you expand your belief and awareness.

Chapter 7 Important Concepts and Exercises

The important concept to understand from this chapter is that creating new beliefs alters your experience of life because it changes your core definition of yourself. Each time you change a belief, you are reborn into a new person with a different experience of life. Rebirth entails a process of exploration as you embody the new world that you have now entered. This is a critical time because your old destructive beliefs will try to pull you back into the old. Stay close to your personal God during this period of transition.

Important Exercises

As you change your beliefs, seek out experiences being the new you. It will feel awkward and scary at first, but you will soon feel comfortable being the new you in a new world. Stay aware of the different way you are experiencing and reacting to life. Don't forget to thank your personal God for the wonderful things happening in your life. Keep saying yes to the new!

CHAPTER 8
Perfection

Bible wisdom: "Therefore you shall be perfect, just as your Father (Parent or personal God) in heaven is perfect" (Matthew 5:48).

What does it mean to be "perfect"? What would your life experience be if you were perfect? Does it mean that you never make mistakes, or think evil thoughts? Does it mean your work desk is always clean and orderly, and your house too? Perfection has nothing to do with what you do, think, or not think. It is about who you are, not what you do! The original meaning of *perfection* is whole, complete, and fully formed. This is how it is used in the Bible and is what you were designed to be. It is about you coming to accept all of yourself, including those parts of you that you hate and believe are bad.

Not that long ago, I had a strange feeling. It occurred to me that I liked my life just as it was right then. I doubted this feeling for a few weeks, thinking it would not last, but it did. I don't remember ever feeling that way about my life. I have always felt that if I just did something spectacular or made a ton of money, then I would be happy with my life. Then the world would finally think me important so I could feel important. No matter what happened, I always felt that it wasn't enough for me to be enough. My current life wasn't enough, but I sure look forward to the day when I finally do enough to feel like I am enough. When I got there, I could relax and be happy and content with my life and with myself.

A Beginner's Guide to Perfection

In my early twenties, when I was struggling with my addiction to alcohol, I remember thinking that if I just got what I saw others having—a house, a family, two cars in the garage, a college degree, a decent career, and some money in the bank—then I would be happy; it would be enough. I sure didn't have anything close to that kind of stuff right now but if I just had that ... Several years later, in my late twenties, when I had a house, a family, two cars in the garage, a college degree, a career, and money in the bank, I remembered those thoughts I had a few years back. I remembered that I had thought all this would make me happy and content, and would be enough. But I was still not happy and content! I felt exactly the same as I felt back then—not enough. The best I could determine was that if I had twice as much, that would do the trick. But something inside me knew this wasn't true; I can always find someone who is bigger, stronger, more intelligent, happier, more respected, or richer. Outer things won't fix inner things.

I derived my life force from the fantasy of one day doing something so spectacular that the fame and riches therefrom would be proof to the world that I was important. The terrible catch was that I couldn't let myself succeed, because then I would have nothing to live for. I would make incredible starts at spectacular things that would have to peter out into failure. I was caught in a hopeless emotional merry-go-round driven by my destructive beliefs about my importance. I was living to die and dying to live. I was unaware about the emotional loop that was driving my life experience and could only attribute my failure to reach my ambitions to an intrinsic defect of my being; I simply was a failure. It was only when my awareness expanded enough that I could see the emotional loop in which I was trapped for what it was. At that point, I could start breaking down the edifice of destructive beliefs in which this destructive emotional loop was built.

What happened to me? Why did I like my life just as it is right now? It's not that I no longer have ambitions in life. I still want to do something great and spectacular in the world. I would love to have a ton of money and be interviewed on the morning talk shows. I still want worldly success in all its worldly forms. All those desires are still there. The big change that has occurred is that I finally accept all of myself, the good and the "bad," the light and the "dark." I have given up trying to reject, fight, and kill off those parts of me that I felt were evil.

Shining the Light on Your Darkness

It is easy to love what we feel is good about ourselves; the hard part is coming to love and accept what we feel is bad about ourselves. As we start challenging our destructive beliefs, we start shining light on our darkness. We start looking at the part of ourselves that we want to keep hidden. We become acutely aware of all the facets that lie hidden in our darkness and develop an intimate relationship with them.

We have spent our entire adult lives feeling ashamed of the dark parts of ourselves. This is a heavy load to carry around in life.

We go to extraordinary lengths to hide our dark side from the world. The fear that somehow the world might discover the part of us that we hate creates an undercurrent of anxiety and stress that permeates our lives. This makes life feel threatening, and so we seek something from outside of ourselves to help us feel better. We make up stories about a future where our darkness has been removed, and we are only that which we feel is good. If I can just get that something or other, be that something or other, my darkness will disappear, and I no longer have to feel the pain of my darkness.

Living life dominated by our destructive beliefs is living under a pall of doom. We put too much faith in the bad things that happen and cannot recognize the many good things in our lives. Our expectations for life are centered on the bad. Our warped expectations of life prevent us from enjoying the many good things that happen in our lives because we must expect that something bad is soon coming. In fact, the better we have it in life, the more powerful is our sense of doom. We don't deserve the good, so it follows that something bad is going to happen to us very soon.

When I shone the light into my darkness, I found many beings. There was the unimportant me, the failure me, the me that is scared of what others think of me, the powerless me, the ugly me, the angry me, the raging me, the indecisive me, the unconfident me, the unlovable me. I hated them all and wished they were dead! I was deeply ashamed of them and certainly never wanted you or anyone else to ever know they existed. When they popped up and showed themselves to others, I would burn with shame and fear. I tried for a long time to kill them off or make them disappear but to no avail. I whipped them, beat them, kicked them, punished them furiously, but there they were, all bloody and bruised, still there. I spent most of my life hating myself because of them.

When I found my personal God, I discovered another side of me. I found the wonderful me, the funny me, the charming me, the confident me, the successful me, the courageous me, the loving and kind me, the me that cared for others, the important me, the me with integrity and honor, the reliable me, the interesting and vibrant me. I liked this side of me and wanted that to be all of me. If I could keep this wonderful side of me and get rid of the other, then I would finally be where I wanted to be. I could then like my life and myself just as I am right now. Then I would be "perfect."

Bible wisdom: "Every kingdom divided against itself is brought to desolation, and every city or house divided against itself will not stand" (Matthew 12:25).

I found myself stuck in perpetual warfare as I kept trying to find a way to kill the parts of me I so hated. Fighting yourself takes a lot of energy and is very exhausting. My ongoing fight with myself drained off much of my energy that could have been used for more constructive purposes. I just didn't know better. I believed that it was my spiritual duty to purge away the parts of me I believed were evil. Why did I believe those parts of me I didn't like were evil? They caused pain! They were a source of shame and embarrassment for me. They proved to me that I was not worthy of being loved, which generated the bulk of my chronic emotional pain.

Integrating, Accepting, and Embracing the Dark

It was around this time in my life that I found the teacher I needed to help me transcend the roadblock of beliefs in which I was stuck. I had come a long way on my own, but now I needed help if I was to get any further. I was a loner who didn't like admitting that I needed help, but I knew that I had reached a point in my spiritual growth where something else was needed if I was to make progress. I signed up with the School of Healing Arts offered through The Estuary in Nashville, Tennessee. I didn't know that I was to find my special teacher there and wasn't really conscious of thinking I needed one. I was simply acting on a deep intuition and longtime desire to enter a school that specialized in this kind of spiritual work. In fact, I was very excited about finally learning how to rid myself of those dark parts of me that I had failed to remove on my own. It was here with my special teacher that I came to understand that I had been trying to do the impossible, trying to be something other than who I am. I never thought that there was light in the dark, or good in the bad, or that the light and dark are inseparable, two sides of the same coin. My teacher also showed me that killing off my darkness is like cutting off my legs. I had been rejecting a part of who I am, which left me only part human, a partial being. The way to solve my problem was to go into the darkness and see it for what it really was, to discover the truth of my whole being! I didn't like this proposition at first, but I trusted my teacher and let her lead me down this path. I am glad I did!

I came to see that I was trying to do the impossible by trying to be something I could not be. I had been trying to deny my humanity by becoming an angel. I thought that if I could transcend my humanity, I could totally live in the spiritual dimension. To do this I had to reject and deny a large part of myself that existed in the emotional and physical dimensions of my personal world. I learned that it is not about forcing myself up to God but about bringing God down into my human-ness, where I experience all of my life, the good and the bad, the light and the dark.

There came a time when I started feeling some compassion for those parts of me that lived in the dark. I came to see that my darkness was part of what makes me who I am. It was difficult, but I started accepting that my darkness was an important and vital part of me. It is what makes me human, which is what I am created to be. God created both the light and the dark parts of me. It wasn't about the good me and the bad me, but about something else, about me being what I am supposed to be—all of me.

I came to see that there was good lurking in my darkness. My destructive belief in my unimportance to life and the world gave me a powerful drive to do something important. This drive gave me creative focus and the confidence that I could do anything that I put my mind to accomplishing. It also honed my ability to develop solutions to problems that were insoluble for others. This drive led to my ability to develop inventions, write patent applications, take and pass the patent bar, and become a registered patent agent with the United States Patent and Trademark Office. It also led to my career in computer and data automation systems. My beliefs in my unimportance propelled me to keep striving for bigger and better things. It was only when I went into the darkness that I could find the goodness that lay therein. When I came to see the goodness in my darkness, my darkness became part of my light.

Integrating, accepting, and embracing the dark parts of ourselves obviates the desperate need to hide, reject, and deny a large part of what makes us who we are. It enables us to shed the burden of shame and fear we carry with us through life. The parts of us of which we are ashamed are disconnected and will keep producing more shame. When we integrate these parts of ourselves, we begin to use their power constructively to help us achieve our true desires in life.

When I started seeing the good in my unimportance, the only thing I changed was my relationship with it. It is still what it is, but instead of it controlling me, I am able to use its power and drive for importance to accomplish things that I want in my life. Being in relationship with it means that I am intimately aware of its power for constructive things, as well as how its power can be used for destructive things. This awareness gives me choice. I can choose to use this power to drive actions I want to take or decide to sit still and take no action. I now have freedom where I had no freedom before. When I was disconnected from these parts of myself, I had no choice because their power could hijack my conscious thoughts and feelings. I simply would believe and so had to act as if they were reality.

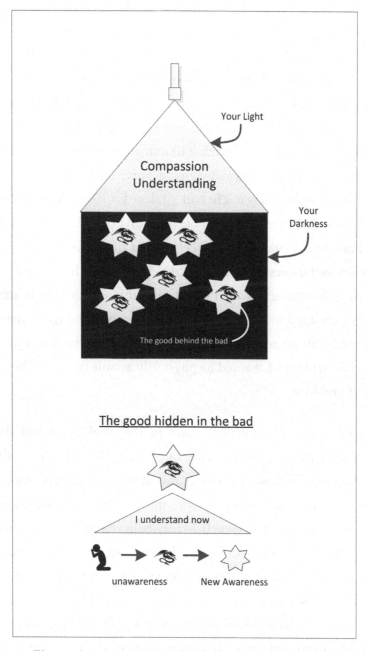

Figure 8.1. Integrating the dark parts of ourselves

In my career, I remember being in a situation where a coworker was trying to control me for his own purposes. Even though he was a peer and worked for the same boss I worked for, he just could not accept that I didn't work for him. This angered me somewhat, which I loved to express whenever I got the chance. He would tell me what to do, and I would remind him that I didn't work for him. He didn't like that one bit and decided to start calling up the boss and saying derisive things about me and my work performance. He had a talent for concocting stories that sounded true but were not. If I didn't obey his command, it became a work performance issue of mine put in terms of sagacious business jargon. One day I got a call from my boss saying that this guy called him saying this and that about me. I got enraged and wanted to kill this guy for saying these untruths about me and my work performance to my boss. I was so mad that I wanted to physically assault the guy when I next saw him.

Luckily, this all took place later in the week, so I had the weekend to stew in my rage and anger. What I was really feeling was the powerlessness that went with my unimportance. But I was now in relationship with my darkness and was curious about why I was so upset. If I truly believed in myself, then I would not care one bit about who said what to whom about me. It came to me that my extreme anger came from a deep feeling of threat and that I have felt this kind of threat before. I stayed curious and kept praying to my personal God for help in the matter and found myself remembering an incident with my older brother when I was ten years old. My brother and I hung out and played with two brothers that lived across the street. We were at their house a lot and so were familiar with their parents. One evening when my family was eating dinner, I made a derogatory comment about our friend's mother. My brother immediately got up from the dinner table and said he was going over to our friend's house and tell their mother what I had just said. I watched him from our kitchen window running over to their house and was terrified. I remembered feeling so powerless to stop him as I watched him running over to their house. This was the deep threat that I was feeling with this guy at work. Now I know why I am so disproportionately upset over this incident with my coworker. It doesn't exonerate his actions, but it did help me see what was happening inside of me.

My rage was impelling me to get violent with this guy, but now I had another choice. I decided that this guy is out of my life and set up a meeting with my boss to discuss the matter. I told my boss that this guy's behavior was unacceptable to me, and either I worked independently of him or found another job. I defended and justified a bit, but stuck with my integrity about what was acceptable and what was not. Because my work was valuable to my boss, I ended up working independently and told this guy to not email or invite me to any of his meetings. A month later, he resigned and went somewhere else.

This was a big change in how I handled problems in my life. When I was not in relationship with my darkness, I would probably have quit my job or ended up being fired for attacking this guy. Being in relationship with my darkness allowed me to use its power and energy to hold my truth and integrity. It certainly was a struggle while the rage was coursing through my being, but I didn't have to surrender to the immense energy of my rage and act destructively. Instead, I channeled the energy into the courage I needed to take the action required to change the situation into one that was acceptable to me.

The evolution in my acceptance of all of me, the light and the dark, is what helped me find contentment and peace within myself and life. It is why I like my life and who I am for the first time in my life. I had made the decision to stop fighting and let myself be all of me, the whole and complete me.

This is what it is to finally be perfect! It is not about being a person that meets cultural, moral, or religious ideals, or only has good days and does good things and thinks good thoughts. It is about honoring and accepting all of who you are and coming to know that God loving you and you loving you are the same thing.

Many years ago, I was on a plane trip to Dallas, Texas, trying to figure out what my special purpose was in life. I had been reading books about this thing called *purpose* and wanted to discover if I had one. I also had been asking my personal God for help in discovering my special purpose in life. My

A Beginner's Guide to Perfection

understanding was that my *purpose* was something that I loved to do and was the special way God worked through me for the good of all God's creation. I had two hours on that plane to Dallas, Texas, and spent that time musing over what, if anything, was my special purpose. I thought about the jobs I had in the past, trying to find a clue to this mysterious *purpose* of mine—nothing stood out. I flipped through some pages of a book I brought with me that had a chapter devoted to the subject and landed on a sentence that said, "Think of something that made your heart sing." This brought back a memory of when I was helping a man trying to recover from his devastating addiction to alcohol and drugs. I was telling him that the "Truth" of him was that he was a perfect, divine child of God and that his problem was that he believed otherwise. He hated himself and believed that he was an unlovable failure of a man. He had done "bad" things in his life, which proved that he was what he believed about himself. I showed him that these were just lies that he believed, and then showed him that he was a perfect, divine child of God by using deductive logic—logic that he could not refute without denying his core beliefs about God. I remember the instant he got it! His eyes lit up like fireworks, and I saw a huge burden fall off his shoulders. He had never considered that the horrible things he thought about himself were untrue. I also showed him how his beliefs about himself were what was keeping him trapped in his drug and alcohol addiction.

David J. Saffold

As I thought about my experience with this man many years ago, I remembered how wonderful I felt when I saw his eyes light up. It made my heart sing! At that very moment, on that plane to Dallas, Texas, I heard a booming voice, the voice of God, tell me that my purpose is to teach the world that they are perfect. This is why I wrote this book! My greatest joy in life is when you stand up and shout to the world with confidence and power, "I am a perfect, divine child of God!"

Chapter 8   Important Concepts and Exercises

The important concept to understand from this chapter is that your relationship with your destructive beliefs has created a house divided against itself. When you change your relationship with your destructive beliefs, you become more whole and complete, more powerful and fully alive to life. You are metamorphosing into a perfect, divine child of God.

Important Exercises

Look within at all the different beings that are you. All of them are your children, even the ones you once felt were bad or evil. Start communing with them and building a relationship with them. If you have faithfully carried out the exercises up to now, then they pose no threat to you. You are the one in charge now. Find the good in each of them and how they help you be the *you* that only you can be. Keep building a relationship with them based on compassion and love.

SUGGESTED READING

Think & Grow Rich, by Napoleon Hill
Sermon on the Mount, by Emmet Fox
The Power of Decision, by Raymond Charles Barker
Ask and It Is Given, by Esther and Jerry Hicks
Discover the Power within You, by Eric Butterworth
The Universe Is Calling, by Eric Butterworth
The Formula, by Vernon M. Sylvest, MD
The Four Spiritual Laws of Prosperity, by Edwene Gaines
The Science of Mind, by Ernest Holmes
The Undefended Self: Living the Pathwork, by Susan Thesenga
Hands of Light: A Guide to Healing through the Human Energy Field, by Barbara Ann Brennan
Light Emerging: The Journey of Personal Healing, by Barbara Ann Brennan

Printed in the United States
By Bookmasters